CW00508708

Looks Like Scunny
Next Season

by

David J. Mooney

Looks Like Scunny
Next Season

by

David J. Mooney

Published in the United Kingdom by Jiggery Pokery 2014.

Copyright © David J. Mooney 2014.

David J. Mooney has asserted his right under the Copyright, Designs and Patents Act 1998 to be identified as the author of this work.

This book is sold subject to the condition that it shall not, by way of trade or otherwise, be lent, resold, hired out, or otherwise circulated without the publisher's prior consent in any form of binding or cover other than that in which it is published and without a similar condition, including this condition, being imposed on the subsequent purchaser.

First published in the United Kingdom in 2014 by Jiggery Pokery.

http://www.davemooney.co.uk
http://www.twitter.com/DavidMooney

No part of this publication may be reproduced, stored in or introduced into a retrieval system, or transmitted, in any form, or by any means (electronic, mechanical, photocopying, recording or otherwise) without the prior written permission of the publisher. Any person who does any unauthorised act in relation to this publication may be liable to criminal prosecution and civil claims for damages.

ISBN: 978-0-9573113-2-9

For Dave

Acknowledgements

It's impossible to have carried out a project as big as this book without the help and support of a whole host of people. Invariably, there will be those I have missed and to them I can only apologise and assure you that it wasn't done out of malice, but rather my own sheer forgetfulness.

My thanks must go to my mum and dad, Helen and Dave Mooney, who have been very supportive throughout the times I've moaned about various problems I've encountered along the way. They have also put me up, clothed me and fed me throughout, too, so I really am eternally grateful.

For help along the way – from contacting all of the former players, through the interviews and to the writing stage – I must also thank Gary James for his always useful advice; Mark Booth, Chris Nield, David Clayton, Chris Bailey, Sharon Latham, Sam Cooke, Les Chapman, Derek Partridge, Peter Barnes and Paul Lake, all from Manchester City and all of whom have helped me track down various members of the squad; Gina Irlam and Howard Burr from City Supporters' Club branches that have allowed me to come along and speak to guests; Matt Diamond and Steve Uttley at Leeds United's and Doncaster Rovers' press offices respectively; Mark Georgevic for helping me speak to one City legend in particular; and Peter Keeling and John Pullan (who allowed me to use their house to write in while they were on holiday).

I must also thank Kev Robinson for being better at spelling and grammar than me and also for continued feedback, help and support; Rob Pollard, Ste Tudor, Paul Sarahs, Simon Curtis and Jamie Whitehead for regular feedback, encouragement and discussions about the book through its various revisions; Adam Carter, and his Twitter page @StatCity, for information and data about the players involved; Dave and Sue Wallace and *King of the Kippax* for support throughout; and George Connor for the idea that I used for the title.

The support from the team that I work with on both *Blue Moon Live* and the *BlueMoon Podcast* has been invaluable, so a huge thanks to Chris Prince, Sam Rosbottom, Paul Atherton, Howard Hockin, Richard Burns and Henry Francis; and, although he's no longer part of the team, I'd also like to thank Dan Burns for his input and support.

Since they were pivotal to this book, I must pay huge thanks to the whole of the Manchester City 1999 Division Two Play-Off Final squad for their patience during the interview process and to the manager, Joe Royle, for helping me contact some of the players and for a very entertaining foreword.

Special thanks also to John from Denton Youth, who didn't tell me his surname because he didn't want to go in the acknowledgements, but I'm too stubborn to let it go and put him in anyway.

About the Book

"It's finished at Sunderland, Manchester United have done all they can, that Rooney goal was enough for the three points... Manchester City are still alive here... Balotelli... Aguero! I swear you'll never see anything like this ever again! So watch it. Drink it in. Two goals in added time for Manchester City to snatch the title away from Manchester United... Stupendous!"

Ask a football fan to talk about last minute Manchester City goals and Martin Tyler's words from Sunday 13 May 2012 will probably be the first that come to mind. For City supporters, however, there are two last minute strikes that hold just as much value – and were arguably more important in the club's history.

Had City lost or drawn with Queens Park Rangers in 2012, the Blues would undoubtedly have challenged for the Premier League title in seasons to come. However, had they lost to Gillingham in the 1999 Division Two Play-Off Final – when they were 2-0 down on 90 minutes, but went on to score twice in stoppage time to pull level – the club may never have recovered from the reaches of the lower leagues.

The Play-Off Final will always hold special memories for City fans. It's always been said that the Blues never do things the easy way and this is one of those games that is always referred to when constructing that argument. As the club has progressed under the ownership of Sheikh Mansour, there was always the concern that the fans wouldn't remember when times were hard – but that was never going to be true.

Back in 1999, City went into the game as the favourites, but not by much. They had faced Gillingham twice that season, drawing 0-0 at Maine Road and winning 2-0 at the Priestfield Stadium, but it wasn't clear-cut as to which side was going to emerge the victor at Wembley.

When Sergio Aguero netted in the 94th minute against QPR, it ended up being a rescue job in a match where City should never have been in the position they were. The fans had turned up to the Etihad Stadium expecting the victory that would win the club's first title in 44 years – of course, they were... City were unbeaten all campaign there, winning 17 and drawing one. And QPR were threatened by relegation.

The comparison comes from the sense of relief the fans experienced. In 2012, supporters were planning on how they would face the world having missed out the title from a seemingly simple position. In the late '90s, they were planning how they'd explain their club messing up on their big day at the national stadium to escape their darkest ever time.

And in both cases, they'd have to hide from United fans: In the earlier, there was City's failure in comparison to the Reds' Champions League win and treble; later, the Blues would have conceded the title to their rivals.

In May 1999, I was 11 years old. I had just finished junior school and had gone through years of jeering and teasing because of how poorly my football team had been performing. Relegations, embarrassing and unexpected defeats, and years of mismanagement culminated in a season in the third tier of English football for the first time. They weren't easy years to follow the club, but the fans kept turning up – maybe it was the hope of a better future or maybe it was the belief that things just couldn't get any worse.

I was on a school trip in Anglesey during the Play-Off Final. Having secured tickets to Wembley, my dad drove from Manchester to pick me up and then continued to London, where we went to the game. At 2-0, I was ready to pick my belongings up and go straight home, missing the rest of the trip.

In the end, my dad drove us home to Manchester after the match and then back to Anglesey the next day, after City came good in the end.

Years later, I was fortunate enough to be able to interview players from the game, having set up the *BlueMoon Podcast* and being part of the *Blue Moon Live* radio show on *Imagine FM*. As the years of the shows went on, I was always trying to track down ex-players to feature on air, until somebody mentioned that 2014 would be 15 years since the Play-Off Final.

Having looked through my book of contacts, I realised I had spoken to a large number of the team already – so I called them one by one and told them my idea. Thankfully, every player from the game agreed to be a part of the book and for that I'm eternally grateful. I met up with them all (but one) – travelling as far south as Ipswich and as far abroad as the Netherlands. Sadly, the USA was out of my budget, so one of the interviews had to be done over the phone.

All of the players gave up a lot of their time to be a part of this book and I feel like they were all in my best interviews in my career. Each was warm and friendly and each was a pleasure to speak to.

I feel especially lucky to have worked with the team I used to watch at Maine Road every week when I was growing up.

I only hope this book does the players and the game justice.

David J. Mooney, 2014

Foreword
by Joe Royle

When I first coined the phrase Cityitis, I never dreamt that it would become ingrained in the minds of the City faithful for years to come. Of course it was always in the DNA of a wonderful friendly club, as Francis Lee had commented many years before that, "If they gave cups for cock ups, the boardroom would be full."

I first joined City as a player on Christmas Eve 1974, as an experienced international with fitness problems and a point to prove. I had a marvellous three-year spell at the club (that was too short), but I had come to love the place and when the chance came to come back as manager, I jumped at it.

Quite honestly, Cityitis has a collection of symptoms that can exasperate, infuriate and elate in equal proportions, and never as prevalent as in the 1998-99 season. Having been relegated on the last day of the previous campaign after winning 5-2 at Stoke, we had to endure the disgrace of playing in the third tier of English football for the first and, definitely now, only time. Of course we would bounce straight back, as we were too big and too good not to... but it wasn't so simple.

The division was waiting for us! A booby trap at some of soccer's outposts, derby games at Stockport and Macclesfield, double defeats to Wycombe and humiliation at York was causing an outbreak of Cityitis in one half of Manchester and great mirth in the other. We were taking a long time to come to terms with a division that was clinging to us like quicksand and slowly dragging us under.

Antibiotics arrived in the shape of Andy Morrison and Ian Bishop, the warrior and the artist, to complement the consistency of Kevin Horlock and Gerard Wiekens, the goals of Shaun Goater, and the spirit of Paul Dickov and Richard Edghill. The recovery was slow but strong and, as the season closed, there was even talk of automatic promotion, but we all knew deep down that that was not the City way.

And so to Wembley. Spirits were high as we prepared for the big day with quiet confidence. We had won convincingly at Gillingham on the run in, so why not? Our arrival at our London hotel was greeted by a storm of tropical proportions. Club clown Kevin Horlock and midfield dynamo Jeff Whitley staged a sit down in the deluge to see who could last the water boarding the longest. Pure nonsense of course, but the team roared with laughter and spirits were high.

Come the day, the game was keenly contested but no classic, and when Carl Asaba put Gillingham ahead with just eight minutes to go it was a hammer blow. Bob Taylor soon added a second goal and I remember turning to Willie Donachie in the closing minutes and saying to him, "It looks like Scunny next season," as Scunthorpe had been promoted in the previous day's play-off.

No sooner had I said it than Kevin Horlock rifled a shot into the corner of the net, surely a consolation only as 90 minutes was showing on the scoreboard.

Adrenalin rose and the records now proclaim that Dicky's goal was the most important in the club's history. Who knows how our fans would have reacted if we lost and stayed down? They had been through thin and thinner with us and were as strained with the situation as much as we were.

Extra time should have been a formality, as Gillingham were exhausted physically and mentally after having victory snatched from them.

But it went to penalties and another outbreak of Cityitis, as Nicky Weaver had given us a fantastic first season but in pre-Wembley practice had not looked a keeper that was a penalty expert and Paul Dickov had been easily our best taker. So Nicky saves two penalties and Dicky hits two posts and misses!

The Oasis anthem was rocking around the ground whilst they celebrated (as only rock stars can) in a private box. The trip home on our coach was mostly quiet with relief, rather than robust with celebration. The season had been long and hard and I found myself smiling as I recalled one of our low points, a defeat at Wycombe, when I had stormed into the dressing room at full time to deliver a necessary meltdown. I was never a ranter or raver but enough was enough. I counted the players in one by one as they went to their seats and sat down in anticipation of a very angry manager. The last one was in and I slammed the door behind them, and paused for effect. As I started, the door fell off its hinges behind me and into the room, the moment had gone and the staff and players were swallowing their giggles.

We're not really here. Well, not anymore.

Joe Royle, 2014

The 1998-99 Season:
The Dark Times

It seems strange to say that the worst day a football club can endure is also the same day that they complete an emphatic victory away from home by five goals to two. However, the reality facing Manchester City fans on the evening of Sunday 3 May 1998 was that the Blues had beaten Stoke at the Britannia Stadium, but had also suffered the ignominy of relegation to their lowest ever point. Before then, in their 104-year history as a league club, City had never kicked a football outside of the top two divisions in England.

The events of Sunday 3 May 1998 confirmed that, come the following August, would no longer be true.

Despite City's win, they needed results elsewhere to go in their favour. Before the match, the Blues were second-bottom of the Division One table, able to overtake three teams: Stoke (their opponents for the final day), Portsmouth and Port Vale – all three were sitting on 46 points, with City on 45. A win for either City or Stoke would only be enough to save them from relegation if one of Portsmouth or Port Vale dropped points. Draws for either weren't enough.

City did their bit, but it would end up being too little too late – as Portsmouth won 3-1 at Bradford, while Port Vale won 4-0 at Huddersfield. It left the Blues in 22nd place, and a point off safety.

Alan Parry, commentating on the game that also saw Stoke relegated, summed it up perfectly: "There'll be a few financial directors rubbing their hands with glee at the thought of visits to Maine Road and visits from Manchester City. We're going to have a league derby next season of Macclesfield against Manchester City – if you'd told anybody that a few years ago, they would have called for the men in the white coats.

"Twice in successive seasons, Manchester City finished in the top six in the Premiership. It was just four or five years ago they were in the top half of the Premiership. Two seasons ago, they went down on the last day, despite drawing with Liverpool.

"Now they find themselves, despite all their efforts today, facing the worst day in their history."

As an image of the away end appears on the screen in second half stoppage time, Parry adds: "It's not the end of the world. It [Division Two] is a decent division; there are some good sides. But you just try telling that to these guys. They've been used to going to Highbury, White Hart Lane, Anfield."

In truth, it had been the culmination of years of mismanagement at City – from board level to the playing staff, nothing had gone right. Relegation from the Premier League in 1996 had been the result of taking just two points from their opening 11 matches. Even then, players had been misinformed that a 2-2 draw at home to Liverpool would be enough to survive and so had begun holding the ball by the corner flag – Coventry and Southampton, both above City on goal difference alone, were also drawing.

By preserving the point at Maine Road, all the Blues were doing was keeping the table exactly as it was – with them in 18th spot and joining QPR and Bolton in the relegation zone at the final whistle.

The plummet through Division One had seen farce at every junction, too: 1996-97 had been the year City were supposed to bounce straight back to the top flight. But three games in, manager Alan Ball resigned and his eventual replacement, Steve Coppell, would last just six matches (33 days) in the job. Frank Clark came in, but City could only stumble to a 14th place finish – 10 points off the play-offs and 19 off automatic promotion. They were nearer to the relegation zone.

At the beginning of 1997-98, *The Times* listed bookmakers' odds that had City as 6/1 joint favourites to win the league. The season culminated in that defeat at Stoke, leaving the club facing the lowest point in their history. The club's top scorer for the campaign managed nine goals. Joe Royle replaced Frank Clark in the February, but as much as he was able to apply the brakes somewhat, there had been too much damage done already.

When August 1998 came around, it would have been very easy for the City fans to have turned their backs on their club. Disaster after disaster had been in the veins of Maine Road and there is only so much heartbreak one can take before they give up hope. However, for the opening day of the season, there was a near-capacity 32,134 fans inside the stadium and they witnessed the new-look City team beat Blackpool by three goals.

Six days later, the fans were brought crashing back down to earth with a 3-0 defeat at Fulham – a game that saw defender Kakhaber Tskhadadze injured for most of the season. It was a blow, as the Georgian had been steadily growing into the team.

Two draws followed – the first with Wrexham finished goalless at Maine Road, while the second (courtesy of a last-minute Shaun Goater effort at Notts County) left the club in their lowest ever league position. With just five points from their opening four games, the Blues sat in

14th in Division Two. On level games with everybody else in the league, they would never drop further.

Form picked up over the course of the next few matches, and the Blues had a three-game winning streak. Walsall and Bournemouth both left Maine Road with nothing, before City went to Macclesfield and brought home three points.

However, talk of a surge in performances was premature. Inconsistency was proving to be a problem, as a run of four draws ended with a defeat at Preston. The bigger picture was worse, too – after that loss, the Blues' win at Wigan was their only victory in eight games and by the end of October, they were floundering in mid-table.

It didn't look like it could get much worse, but defeat at Wycombe was followed by draws with Gillingham, Luton and Bristol Rovers. After 21 matches, the Blues had won just seven. Questions about the manager's position were beginning to be raised and they weren't answered when defeat at York left the club 15 points off the top.

Colin Jonas, writing on the mcivta.com blog was stinging in his criticism of the side: "Our only hope is that a good run might see us into the play-offs, but my main concern is that we're only nine points above the relegation positions. Surely we're too good to go down again, but who knows while Royle and Donachie remain in charge?"

What none of the fans were to know, however, was that the Blues were to embark on a fantastic run of form. After that defeat at Bootham Crescent on Saturday 19 December 1998, City would lose just two more matches all season. It would have needed a miracle for the club to win automatic promotion from that position, but had the campaign been just a few games longer they might well have done it. In the end, they finished five points off second place.

The game that seemingly kicked the Blues into gear was a narrow victory over Wrexham at the Racecourse Ground. By all accounts the visitors had played poorly and could quite easily have fallen behind but for some cracking saves by Nicky Weaver from Wrexham's loan signing, Terry Cooke. Cooke would go on to sign for City later in the season.

In the second half, a goal from Gerard Wiekens broke the deadlock and it was enough for City to win, combined with several more good saves from Weaver.

The real kick-starter for the season, though, came five minutes from time in the very next game. After falling behind to Stoke at Maine Road, Paul Dickov equalised midway through the second half. It had looked like it was going to be another frustrating game for the Blues and another home draw to boot, but with a few minutes remaining, Gareth Taylor rose to nod home and seal the club's first back-to-back wins in almost two months. Over the next 21 games, City lost once.

A bad run came at exactly the wrong time for the club. With three games to play, City were two points behind second placed Walsall. A defeat at home to Wycombe and a draw at Bristol Rovers left the Blues seven points off promotion and in 4th going into the final game, meaning they knew a win against York could only lift them to 3rd. And that's exactly where they finished.

Seven days after that final game of the season, the Blues faced Wigan in their first leg of the play-off semi-finals. It couldn't have got off to a worse start: with just seconds on the clock, a mix-up between Wiekens and Weaver allowed Stuart Barlow in to score. A Dickov equaliser (and away goal) rescued the tie for the Blues, before a dubious maybe-it-was-handball-but-nobody-could-really-tell goal from Shaun Goater in the second leg was enough to secure a game at Wembley.

Even then, though, City didn't do things the easy way. They never do.

		W	D	L	F	A	Pts	Home	Away
1	Fulham	31	8	7	79	32	101	3-0	0-3
2	Walsall	26	9	11	63	47	87	3-1	1-1
3	**Man City**	22	16	8	69	33	82		
4	Gillingham	22	14	10	75	44	80	0-0	2-0
5	Preston N End	22	13	11	78	50	79	0-1	1-1
6	Wigan Athletic	22	10	14	79	48	76	1-0	1-0
7	Bournemouth	21	13	12	63	41	76	2-1	0-0
8	Stoke City	21	6	19	59	63	69	2-1	1-0
9	Chesterfield	17	13	16	46	44	64	1-1	1-1
10	Millwall	17	11	18	52	59	62	3-0	1-1
11	Reading	16	13	17	54	63	61	0-1	3-1
12	Luton Town	16	10	20	51	60	58	2-0	1-1
13	Bristol Rovers	13	17	16	65	56	56	0-0	2-2
14	Blackpool	14	14	18	44	54	56	3-0	0-0
15	Burnley	13	16	17	54	73	55	2-2	6-0
16	Notts County	14	12	20	52	61	54	2-1	1-1
17	Wrexham	13	14	19	43	62	53	0-0	1-0
18	Colchester Utd	12	16	18	52	70	52	2-1	1-0
19	Wycombe W.	13	12	21	52	58	51	1-2	0-1
20	Oldham Athletic	14	9	23	48	66	51	1-2	3-0
21	York City	13	11	22	56	80	50	4-0	1-2
22	Northampton Tn	10	18	18	43	57	48	0-0	2-2
23	Lincoln City	13	7	26	42	74	46	4-0	1-2
24	Macclesfield Tn	11	10	25	43	63	43	2-0	1-0

Manchester City 2-2 Gillingham (3-1 pens)

Sunday 30 May 1999, Wembley Stadium
Referee: Mark Halsey
Attendance: 76,935 (Division Two Play-Off Record)

Manchester City: Weaver, Crooks (Taylor 85), Edghill, Wiekens, Morrison (c) (Vaughan 63), Horlock, Brown (Bishop 63), Whitley, Dickov, Goater, Cooke
Goals: Horlock (90), Dickov (90+5)
Booked: Wiekens, Taylor
Sent Off: -
Manager: Joe Royle

Gillingham: Bartram, Southall, Ashby, Smith, Butters, Pennock, Patterson (Hodge 105), Hessenthaler (c), Asaba (Carr 87), Galloway (Saunders 56), Taylor
Goals: Asaba (81), Taylor (87)
Booked: Taylor, Carr
Sent Off: -
Manager: Tony Pulis

Following an end of season surge up the table, City had finished the 1998-99 campaign in third place in Nationwide League Division Two. Gillingham, meanwhile, had been hot on their tails, ending the season a mere two points behind the Blues. Both teams, disappointed in not making the automatic promotion positions, dusted themselves down and got on with their jobs in the play-offs.

City, despite falling behind in the opening seconds at Springfield Park, came back to beat Wigan Athletic over two legs – bringing a 1-1 draw back to Maine Road, where the Blues went on to beat the Latics 1-0 thanks to a dubious Shaun Goater goal. In the other match, Gillingham did exactly the same – leaving Preston with a 1-1 draw and beating their opponents 1-0 when back in Kent.

As both sets of fans headed towards Wembley, they took a drenching, as the heavens opened. Nerves were brimming over and tensions were high. The City fans knew the pressure was on for the club: nobody wanted another season in the lowest tier that the club had ever featured in and, in truth, it could have been disastrous for the financial situation.

On top of that, a mere four days earlier, rivals Manchester United had lifted the Champions League. If City were ever going to recover as a force in England, it surely had to begin today. Meanwhile, for Gillingham, promotion would have seen the club reach the highest position in their history. Both sides had a lot to play for.

It was City in their change strip of lurid yellow and dark blue that got the game underway and immediately they were on the attack. Dickov, as tenacious as ever, wriggled his way into the Gillingham box and tried to work an opening. As he tried to flick it past Ashby, the defender lifted his elbow and knocked the ball directly into the air, while Dickov ended in a heap. Bartram collected the loose ball and the City players cried for a penalty. There was nothing doing from referee Mark Halsey, just 20 seconds into the game.

It was a frantic start as both sides looked for the early advantage, and perhaps the greasy surface was playing its part in upping the tempo. A free kick routine allowed Butters to shoot from 30 yards and, though Weaver threw himself towards his right hand post, the effort swung away from the target. Whitley responded with a similar effort six minutes later, though with much the same outcome.

Weaver was forced into his first good save of many throughout the game, as Gillingham broke on ten minutes. A cross from the right wing missed everybody and bounced for Galloway to turn and shoot at goal. It was heading for the top corner, but the young City keeper got up well to palm it behind with both hands.

City seemed to settle the quicker. Crooks tried a low drive from long range that was just inches from beating Bartram at the foot of his right hand post, before more dogged Dickov hard work gifted his side another chance on goal. Morrison cleared a Bartram goal kick with a powerful header downfield, which Goater was able to flick towards the little Scot. Chasing it down, he pressured Southall into a mistake and Cooke nicked it from him. A good cross to the unmarked Horlock should have opened the scoring, but the midfielder's header was well saved by Bartram, low to his right.

Eight minutes before half time, Gillingham had the ball in the net on the breakaway. However, an offside flag from the assistant put a quick end to the celebrations, as Asaba had drifted beyond the line of the defence before Robert Taylor played it into the middle.

The second half was much cagier, as both teams were seemingly aware that any mistake could be costly. On the hour mark, Goater was close to connecting to a loose ball inside the box following a Horlock free kick that had been aimed at Morrison, but a toe-end from Pennock got it away and left the Bermudian swinging at thin air.

A poor clearance from Edghill on his weaker side almost gifted Gillingham a chance inside the box. Southall crossed from the right and

Saunders flung himself towards the ball to connect with a diving header. Weaver was helpless, but he wasn't needed in the end, as the effort flashed across the face of goal and skidded behind.

With 20 minutes to play, a square ball across the City box allowed Smith to smash a low drive towards goal. It was straight at Weaver and he got his body behind it, so while the fans might have had their hearts in their mouths when it spilled from his grasp, but there was no real danger of it slipping over the line as he got back to recover.

It was City who came closest to breaking the deadlock as Edghill found Dickov on the counter, following a good tackle from the defender. Face to face with Hessenthaler, he slowed down and allowed Cooke to make the run on the overlap. The winger received it and then crossed to find Goater unmarked at the back of the box and, with a deft side-footed touch, he took aim for the bottom corner. The striker beat Bartram but not the post, and it rebounded back into play.

But the game was becoming stretched. As soon as City should have been in front, it was Gillingham who had a golden opportunity to open the scoring. A missed header by Wiekens forced Weaver to leave his area to clear. But on his wrong foot, the City keeper smashed the ball only as far as Robert Taylor and, with an open goal, the striker had a go from 40 yards. He missed the target, as Weaver scrambled back.

As the game headed for the final ten minutes, it was City beginning to pile on the pressure. Dickov smashed a low cross through the six-yard box, but, despite desperate dives from Goater and Horlock, nobody could touch it in. A good claim by Weaver then allowed City to break and, as Dickov found Cooke, the winger's shot from the edge of the area was neatly flicked over the bar by Bartram.

Despite the pressure, though, the deadlock was finally broken by Gillingham. Smith held up the ball under pressure from Wiekens and found Asaba running clear. Through on goal, his toe poke found the roof of the net, right in front of his own fans. With nine minutes to play, it gave the Kent side the advantage.

City could have collapsed: immediately from kick-off, Gillingham were back on the attack and the ball broke for Robert Taylor to volley at goal. It was destined for the top corner but for a wonderful fingertip save from Weaver, who redirected it onto the post and behind.

Equally, though, Gillingham were thankful for Bartram's left foot, as he blocked an effort from Dickov from inside the six-yard box, as City began to throw bodies forward. Edghill drove the ball into the area and it found the Scot unmarked, but the goalkeeper used his boot to keep out the side-footed effort.

With just over three minutes until stoppage time, it looked all over.

Asaba held the ball up before back-heeling it into the path of the oncoming Robert Taylor. He powered around Vaughan and smashed a shot past Weaver and into the back of the net. City hearts sank, the Gills in dreamland.

There were a mere 15 seconds left on the clock when the City fans were given a brief moment of hope. With stoppage time to come, a step-over from Gareth Taylor allowed Dickov to flick the ball through for Goater. Just as he was about to pull the trigger, he was tackled by a combination of two defenders and the goalkeeper. As the ball broke to Horlock, it left him with an open goal and he drove it first time into the back of the net.

The board went up and showed five additional minutes. Tony Pulis fumed, while the City players grabbed the ball and raced back to halfway and both sets of fans anxiously set about chewing their fingernails.

There was only a minute to play when Wiekens received the ball from a throw in on the halfway line. Gillingham had dropped deep into their own area, protecting their slender advantage and the defender lumped it forward – there was little time for anything else. A flick from Gareth Taylor fell to Horlock, who prodded it to Goater. Once again, he was tackled as he tried to pull the trigger, but the loose ball slid through to Dickov.

He took a touch to open up his body and, falling backwards, swung his boot to unleash the shot. Despair in the stands behind the goal suddenly turned to delight. Bartram couldn't get his hand up in time to block and the ball hit the top corner of the net. The Scot peeled away and slid across the Wembley turf, closely followed by his teammates. The fans behind lost their cool, as relief swept over them. At the other end, Gillingham heads dropped.

There were 50 seconds of stoppage time to play when the ball crossed the line. Extra time beckoned.

Having switched formations, extra time found City dominant but struggling to break through. The Blues – now playing three centre-backs and three forwards – faced a Gillingham side that had replaced a striker with a defender in order to hang on to their original lead.

Goater couldn't force the ball towards goal as it was driven through the box, before Vaughan's header flashed over the bar as he tried to redirect a miscued Whitley shot.

With 20 minutes of extra time played, it was nearly another disaster for City, as a clearance was charged down and fell nicely for Robert Taylor. Weaver was quickly off his line to flick it away with his arm, but it landed only as far as Hodge. The goalkeeper, though, blocked his effort with his boot.

It was becoming frantic again as, less than a minute later, Dickov found himself free inside the Gillingham box, but his header from a cross from the left was straight at the goalkeeper. Bartram held it, though either side of him and it would have put City ahead for the first time in the game.

If City felt aggrieved about the handball in the opening seconds of the match, they were soon on the receiving end of a piece of good fortune. Whitley came sliding in to block a low cross from Hodge and it hit his arm before bouncing behind. City were lucky that the referee only pointed for a corner and not for a penalty.

Neither side were able to force another good chance in the time remaining and the game went to penalties.

City, who had been on the front foot thanks to those two late goals, had the advantage of taking the kicks in front of their own fans. Horlock made the long walk, before sending Bartram the wrong way.

A wall of noise faced Smith as he stepped up to take the first Gillingham kick. He went for pace and power, smashing it straight down the middle of the goal. Weaver went the wrong way, but he stuck out a foot to block the ball and stop it from crossing the line. He turned to the celebrating fans and threw a fist into the air. It was advantage City.

City's next kick was remarkable. Paul Dickov, faced by the best man at his wedding, Vince Bartram, sent the keeper the wrong way. The kick hit the inside of the right hand post, travelled right across the goal-line to hit the inside of the left hand post and bounce out. It didn't go in.

The miss wasn't costly for City, though. Adrian Pennock couldn't hit the target, as his kick left Weaver rooted in the centre of his goal. It was high and wide and City still had the upper hand, especially as Terry Cooke put the Blues in full control of the shootout. Bartram went the correct was for his spot-kick, but it was powerful and right in the bottom corner of the goal, meaning the keeper just couldn't get across to it in time.

Gillingham's third kick fell to John Hodge. If there was to be any hope of a reprieve for the Kent side, he had to score. He did, coolly slotting the ball into the top corner of the goal, as Weaver chose the wrong direction. But it was a case of 'anything you can do' for City's next taker – and there will have been eyebrows raised from the stands, as Richard Edghill came jogging forward. He'd never scored a senior goal, but nevertheless he hit the underside of the bar and found the net. A kiss of the badge told the fans what it meant.

It also meant the next kick was crucial. Guy Butters stepped up knowing that he had to score or it was game over. He tried a powerful shot straight down the middle, but Weaver chose correctly. Diving to his left, he parried it with both hands, before setting off on a wild run around the Wembley turf.

City were back from the dead. Seconds away from staying in Division Two and with some of the fans having left, believing they'd seen it all before, they performed the rescue job of all rescue jobs. Despair became delight.

The rebuilding of the club had started.

1 NICKY WEAVER

"Hi Nicky." I said into my mobile, as I struggled for signal in a remote area of Sheffield. I'd agreed to meet the former City keeper at his house, but had been somewhat delayed by a combination of road closures and average speed checks. "I'm on your road now," I said, "but I can't for the life of me find where you are."

The road has a bizarre numbering system for its houses: it does not have a numbering system for its houses. Number one is followed by number three is followed by The Old Farm House is followed by The Stables is followed by number seventeen is followed by number forty-four is followed by The Grange.

After a few minutes of searching, Nicky came to the end of his drive, just as I'd pulled in on the road. I straightened my rather rushed parking job and made my way over. He invited me in and we sat down in a quiet corner of his house to begin, getting down to business with his first year as City's number one.

"I was there the previous season," he says, about the 1997-98 campaign. "I travelled a bit with the first team and I think I was on the bench twice. I just played in the reserves and they used to have an A Team then and I was playing in that. And then they were relegated, which probably helped me to get a chance. Tommy Wright was the first choice goalkeeper, him and Martyn Margetson.

"Martyn Margetson left and I went back for preseason just thinking Tommy would start. I'd done okay in preseason and Joe Royle put me in."

Weaver's debut came in a 3-0 win over Blackpool at Maine Road. Goals from Shaun Goater, Lee Bradbury and Kakhaber Tskhadadze won the game, while, at the back, the Blues were more solid and secure than they had been in years. Granted, it was a lower standard of football, but it was still refreshing for the fans to see.

"I ended up playing 55 games that year," Weaver remembers, "and

CITY CAREER STATS

Apps: 207 (2 sub)
Goals: 0

Signed: April 1997
Left: July 2007

Debut: Blackpool (h), 1998
Result: 3-0 victory

that was the most I've ever played in a season. I really enjoyed it and although it was only League One as it is now, it was a massive platform to play in front of 28-30,000 people at Maine Road."

While Weaver's performances that year were attracting the plaudits, the team's fortunes weren't going quite as well. The 3-0 opening day victory was quickly followed by a 3-0 defeat at Craven Cottage. Two draws then followed: 0-0 with Wrexham at home and 1-1 at Notts County.

It got worse, too. From September to December 1998, the Blues went on a run of just three wins in 15 games, a spell that included seven draws. And it was the draws doing the damage as, after losing at York on 19 December, City found themselves languishing in 12th place in the league – 15 points off the summit.

"But then everything turned around," the goalkeeper says. "We signed Andy Morrison. The Goat started firing. In the last 23 games, we only lost something like three and ended up finishing third."

I checked the results afterwards – it was actually two defeats in 24.

"For me looking back now, as a young kid who'd played one game at Mansfield Town, to start playing every week for City and become the number one there was, at the time, something I didn't probably appreciate. Now, though, I look back with great fondness."

When it came to the play-offs at the end of the 1998-99 season, the Blues were the form team in the league. Their late surge up the table hadn't been enough to earn them an automatic place, but it meant they were ready for the semi-finals. Though, on travelling to Wigan's Springfield Park, City got off to the worst possible start.

"Yeah, I remember it," Weaver chuckles when I ask what happened, "the ball came back and I shouted. I wanted to clear it, so I shouted, 'Keeper's!' to Gerard [Wiekens]. But then I thought he shaped like he was going to clear it. So I backed off thinking he was going to take matters into his own hands, which would have been fine. But he sort of stepped over it and I've stepped back. And I think it was Stuart Barlow who's nipped in and put it in after something like 20 seconds."

Paul Dickov eventually equalised for the visitors and, in the return leg, Shaun Goater bagged the winner, sending the Blues to Wembley and cueing a pitch invasion at full time.

For a young lad of just 20 years old, how was he feeling before the game? Anxious? Nervous? Worried?

"Excited!" he almost shouts, "I was rooming with Lee Crooks. We all had some club suits. They weren't the best in the world, but we all looked relatively smart. I remember the coach journey there and seeing all the City fans all over. Once we got to Wembley Way, it was just a sea of blue.

"I remember walking out – we used to walk out behind one of the goals – and looking over my left shoulder, my mum and dad and everyone was up there..." His thoughts trail off as he tries to remember the game itself, "I remember making a save early on to my right hand side at my near post," he says, demonstrating with his hands, "it was probably not the best game in the world to watch as a neutral until about ten minutes to the end."

Weaver admits to thinking it was over when Robert Taylor scored Gillingham's second goal of the day, with only three minutes plus stoppage time remaining. He'd had no chance with the first goal from Carl Asaba, but for the second he was perhaps eager off his line to try and make the save to set up another attack.

"But," he adds, "I always remember that I got the ball out of the net as quickly as I could and got it back to the halfway line. I remember just saying, 'Come on' because we'd just seen what United had done."

"I always remember that I got the ball out of the net as quickly as I could and got it back to the halfway-line..."

The week earlier, Manchester United had been crowned winners of the Champions League, thanks to two late goals. It was a world away from where the Blues were at the time.

"It only takes a second to score a goal," Weaver continues, before talking about City's first. "It was a good finish, actually. He [Horlock] had a bit to do with it; it wasn't just a tap in. And then the biggest thing was when the fourth official held up five minutes. They'd taken their forwards off and put defenders on. And when it broke to Dicky it was just unbelievable.

"But we had to calm ourselves down. Then extra time came and went without a lot happening..." as his voice trails off as he tries to think back, I take the opportunity to ask him about some of his saves from the game – especially one at 1-0, where he tipped a Robert Taylor shot onto the post.

"Did I do a bad clearance?" he asks, "I think I left-footed a clearance and I think it might have just gone wide. Or did I touch it onto the post? Did I touch one onto the post?" Over the years, the two incidents have merged into one in Weaver's memory. The open goal – from his left-footed clearance – dropped wide in extra time, while his fingertip save onto the post came seconds after Gillingham had opened the scoring, "I haven't seen the game for ten years!" he laughs.

"I remember as well that there was nothing I could do, but I just really wanted to get involved," he says. Joe Hart expressed a similar view in the next 'back from the dead' game, as City scored two stoppage time goals against QPR some 13 years later. "I was just hoping that we'd get that one chance and thankfully we did."

It's difficult to avoid coming back to that goal: "I never really knew if it took a deflection. I think it took the slightest deflection. And when it went into that net, I remember running and diving on my belly.

"When we went into the huddle after full time," he continues, "we were elated and they must have been... they'd taken their forward players off, so all they could do was defend, really."

A grin begins to appear on the goalkeeper's face as we get towards talking about penalties. By Weaver's own admission, he couldn't have lost in that situation. Nobody expects the goalkeeper to save a penalty, so by this stage the pressure was off him entirely.

"I think the biggest thing for us was getting the penalty kicks at our end," he says, "you wouldn't have fancied taking a penalty. Certainly not when you've got all the noise from the City fans behind that goal.

"Fortunately, I saved the first one. Everyone says that [it hit his trailing leg], but it didn't. As I dived, I've taken my left foot towards the ball and kicked it, rather than it hitting my leg.

"They missed the second one. I think they scored the third one and then it got to the position where I remember saying to the linesman, 'If I save this, is that it?' and he went, 'Yeah.' And I said, 'Are you *sure*?' And he went, 'Yeah.' I knew Shaun Goater was taking the next one and I didn't really fancy him.

"I picked my side and dived," he says about saving the shot. "But I'd had a stinker that week in training. Dicky was just going for the same corner every time and just hitting it, so even when I knew where [it was going] – without going stupidly early – it was just like a tennis ball machine and going in the corner every time. We practised every day after training and I just didn't really get near any."

But what about the celebrations after that final stop?

"I don't know why I went on that silly run," he says, "youthful exuberance or something... I just didn't want that moment to end, I think. I just kept running and

"I remember saying to the linesman, 'If I save this, is that it?' and he went, 'Yeah.' And I said, 'Are you *sure*?' And he went, 'Yeah.'..."

eventually Andy Morrison stopped me and there was a mass pile-on. I think my words were, 'Get off, you fat bastard!'

"I'd just ran and ran and ran. The lads piled on and I just couldn't breathe!"

Weaver was quickly becoming something of a fans' favourite at Maine Road. A season of good performances – in which he broke the club's record for the number of clean sheets racked up in one campaign – was followed by another, where he went from cult hero to England Under-21 star.

And for the club, there were back-to-back promotions.

"We were delighted. Don't forget we'd only finished third the previous year," the goalkeeper says, "it's not like we'd run away with the league. We added Mark Kennedy, who was a big signing for us and he had a great year that year. Danny Granville came and he did well.

"We didn't sign loads of players, but we just kind of rode the crest of the wave. We'd go to places like Birmingham and win 1-0. I remember going to [Crystal] Palace and winning, Nottingham Forest and winning. We just used to go to places and win! And we just had this habit of winning!"

I think it's partly Weaver's thick South Yorkshire accent, but mainly the unexpectedness of City's success in just his second full season, but the pitch in his voice keeps getting higher.

The praise for the young keeper was still very forthcoming. One match in particular stands out, as City took on promotion rivals Ipswich at Maine Road. Down one end was Richard Wright (who would go on to sign for City as a veteran under Roberto Mancini), who was Weaver's rival in the England Under-21s.

With neither goalie willing to be outdone by the other, some of the saves on display were phenomenal. City won the game 1-0 and Weaver won the battle, with one ludicrous double stop, before diving on another shot on the line when the Ipswich players had already started celebrating the goal.

"I think I only missed one league game that season, I think I had 'flu or something" he recalls. "To play a big part in that season – and it was only my second, so after two years I was thinking, 'Ah, this is alright!' – and for it to end at Blackburn, in some ways it was more remarkable than Wembley.

"We had equally as many fans outside the ground as we did in it. They hit the woodwork three or four times. I've made a couple of saves... Alan Kelly was in their goal and he never had a shot to save!

"We were 1-0 down at half time, Matt Jansen had scored. And Ipswich were beating Walsall, so everything that could go wrong was going wrong. I remember... I'm sure it was Ashley Ward who hit the post. I'm beaten and I've turned around and it's just come straight back to me. And that's when you're thinking, 'We can't lose!'"

His voice is going high again.

"We had three shots, scored three and they scored an own goal. It was staggering.

"We went out onto the balcony and the fans were outside and, again, I'm only 21. And I remember we went to the Midland Hotel after for all the celebrations and stuff. I was sat down with Ian Bishop.

"We'd had a couple of drinks and he's saying, 'Make the most of it, this doesn't happen every year,' and I'm thinking, 'Yeah, what does he know?' And now I find myself that older lad telling the younger ones that this all seems like two minutes ago. And they're looking at me like I looked at Bish that day!"

Promotion to the Premier League, though, was where things started to get tough for both City and their goalkeeper. Wins were harder to come by and, for a team that had been used to long unbeaten spells, it was a shock to the system. Between the end of October and the end of February, the Blues won just once in 17 matches. That run included a spell of six consecutive defeats.

Weaver is very honest in his assessment of that season: "We weren't ready, looking back now. We started off okay, but we lost to Manchester United and we took a battering at Arsenal. And once you get down there in the Premier League, those winter months are tough.

"I felt I started off okay, but then I had a dip in form. Looking back, it'd have been nice if the manager could have pulled me out and put someone else in. I could have done with coming out for four or five games and then going back in a bit fresher.

"I felt under pressure," he says, "the teams that get relegated don't score enough goals, so we obviously didn't score enough. So that puts more pressure on the back lads because you know if you concede, we're not going to score two or three."

Around that time, there were reports surfacing in newspapers that the City players had been swept up in what had become known as a 'drinking culture' at the club.

Weaver disagrees: "Listen, we used to go out a lot. We've got no qualms about that. We didn't go out any more than when we'd been promoted the year before – so it suddenly went from 'team spirit' to a 'drink culture'. Then we get into the Premier League and we're losing a few games and we still went out.

"It gets magnified a bit and the press love all of that. I was in the paper a few times and it sort of marred what had happened over the previous two years.

"People had said to me, 'I saw you out at 4am before a game!' and I always thought, 'I don't think you have... you might have seen me out at 4am after a game.' So people stick 20 per cent on it. Looking back, it was just really disappointing. I think more so for the gaffer because it always stuck with him then.

"We just went up too early. It was disappointing and we sort of whimpered out at the end. It was a bit sad really, because Joe [Royle] got sacked and after everything he'd done. I felt really sorry for him because he's my favourite manager I've ever played with. I had possibly my best spell under him."

Weaver was dropped towards the end of his first Premier League season. In his place, the manager opted for new signing Carlo Nash. It wasn't enough to keep the team in the division, but it perhaps did ease the pressure on him and take him out of the spotlight.

However, his future was uncertain with a new manager coming in. As Kevin Keegan took the reins at Maine Road, fortunes took a turn for the worse for Weaver. Already unsure as to whether he would be first choice for the season, he picked up a thigh injury in preseason and was forced to miss the start.

"People had said to me, 'I saw you out at 4am before a game!' and I always thought, 'I don't think you have... you might have seen me out at 4am after a game.'"

When I ask whether he felt confident of being Keegan's number one, he wasn't sure: "I think I'd have started the season, I'm not 100 per cent sure. I might be wrong on that one."

In the end, Carlo Nash began the season between the sticks. Weaver wasn't fit for the bench in the opener against Watford and instead it was youngster Brian Murphy who took the goalkeeping spot in the substitutes. He was, however, back in action sooner than probably expected – as he came on for the injured Nash in the next game at Norwich.

Though having got into the starting line-up, by his own admission, Weaver found it difficult to build up a rhythm, as Kevin Keegan seemingly couldn't decide who his first choice was: "He sort of swapped us about a bit that season. You'd go in for seven or eight games and think you're doing alright and then he'd suddenly say, 'Nicky, I'm going to put Nashy in on Saturday.'

"But then Nashy would go in and do alright, and then he'd pull me and say, 'You're playing Saturday.' I remember playing away at Ipswich in the cup and Nashy had been playing and doing okay. He just pulled me and said he was playing me.

"So he was just trying to keep it fresh and we probably played about the same number of games that year."

But then, on Tuesday 5 March 2002, Weaver's world was turned upside down. City travelled to Birmingham looking to add to their title credentials. In the 33rd minute, the keeper went off with a seemingly innocuous injury.

"Someone shot and it was just going wide. I've just dived – I knew it was going wide, so it was just to cover it. As I landed, I felt something funny in my right knee. I got up and I put the ball down for the goal kick and I'm thinking, 'I can't kick this...'"

"Someone shot and it was just going wide. I've just dived – I knew it was going wide, so it was just to cover it. As I landed, I felt something funny in my right knee. I got up and I put the ball down for the goal kick and I'm thinking, 'I can't kick this...'

"So I've tried to kick it and I think I've hit it straight out. I came off and I went for a scan the next day. I'd just torn my cartilage, which is about five or six weeks and a routine sort of thing. So I went and had this operation thinking I'd be back before the end of the season.

"They said it had been successful. I rehabbed it. Just as I was about to go back into training, my knee ballooned up."

I get the impression that it's still difficult for Weaver to talk about. From the excitable Nicky Weaver earlier in the day, he'd become quieter and all the more serious. His eyes began to well up slightly as he remembered what had happened over ten years ago.

He tells me that he went through the same process once more: another operation and another programme of rehabilitation. Just with the first time, as he was getting ready to start training again, the swelling returned.

"That's when alarm bells started to ring and I was thinking, 'There's something not right here,'" Weaver says. "I remember going for a walk around the training ground with the physio at Carrington and he was saying, 'We don't know what's up with your knee, Nicky.'

"You ask a physio how long you're going to be out for and he can tell you. But he was saying, 'We've been in there twice and we haven't sorted the problem out. We don't know what...'"

His voice trails off, while he takes a moment.

"Paulo Wanchope had just been over to Cleveland, Ohio. There's a place there called The Cleveland Clinic and that's where the Costa Rican national team used. And he said they were really good. Alfie Haaland had been as well, so I went over there.

"I had another operation over there. They did touch on this big operation I might have to have, but there were other procedures they had to go through first," he says. But, as with the previous two attempts at sorting the problem out, Weaver felt like it was the same old story – he came home to complete his rehabilitation and, just when he was about to start training, it blew up once more.

Now back at square one for the third time, Weaver flew back to the States to have yet another operation. "I actually got back into training this time," he says. "I made the bench a few times. I played in the UEFA Cup against TNS at Cardiff – that was the only game I played for a few years. I got back for quite a while this time, but then it went again.

"So this was when I was thinking, 'This could be it for me now'. I'd had four operations in round about a year and I'd not played. I'd hardly trained. I was only 23 or 24 at this point."

Knowing that the situation was getting worse, Weaver contacted The Cleveland Clinic once again. He explained that the operation they had originally talked about was to have a dead man's cartilage implanted into his knee, a procedure that wasn't done in Europe. He met the conditions needed for the surgery too – his knee was in a bad way, but not so far gone that it wasn't saveable.

"I had to go on a donors' list," he remembers. "They knew exactly what they needed. We were waiting for somebody to die, almost. It needed to be someone of a similar size and build and of a similar age.

"I got the phone call over Christmas, because I went in early January. They gave me a 70-30 chance of it being a success. And, I'll never forget, I went there with Jim Webb [City's physio at the time] and we were sat down in the waiting room when this guy walked in. He was in all sorts of pain and he sat next to us. I said to him, 'You look like you're struggling,' and he said, 'Yeah, I had a meniscal transplant last year.'

"And that was exactly what I was having."

Despite the worries, the doctor was optimistic. The operation was deemed a success and Weaver's body didn't reject the new cartilage. And, once again, he was back on the rehabilitation trail.

"The luckiest thing for me was that, just before I got injured, I'd signed a new four and a half year deal. So I had time on my side. Obviously, the club had the money to send me over to America so I'll always be grateful to City for that and I'll always feel lucky that I had length on my contract.

"I was on crutches for six weeks. I was on a walking stick at 24. I didn't have a drink for a year. I needed to get it right and if I didn't and never played again, I needed to know that I'd done everything I possibly could to get right."

"I was on crutches for six weeks," he says, "I was on a walking stick at 24. I packed the drink in. I didn't have a drink for a year. I thought I needed to get it right and if I didn't and never played again, I needed to know that I'd done everything I possibly could to get right. So I lived like a monk for a year.

"I was going swimming on a Saturday night when the lads were going out.

"And then a year down the line, I ended up playing a reserve game against Blackburn down at Morecambe. I thought I'd never play again, so I was buzzing to be back. And then I ended up going out on loan."

But it wasn't all plain sailing for the goalkeeper. Just when things were looking up again, Weaver remembers there was more misfortune for him: "I ended up getting back and then I broke my wrist! Joey Barton cracked a shot in training; I saved it and bent my wrist back. I'd cracked a bone and needed an operation on that.

"I ended up going on loan to Sheffield Wednesday and I did ok. I sort of found my feet," he says. But he wasn't sure about his future at City, as things had changed somewhat at the club. Kevin Keegan had resigned and Stuart Pearce was now the boss.

"I was in the last year of my contract by this stage and Stuart Pearce offered me another year. I think I ended up playing 31 games in my last year [2006-07]. For me, although Wembley and the two promotions were the stand-out moments, I feel my biggest achievement was getting back and playing back in the Premier League.

"The club doctor had to write letters to my insurers telling them where I was at. It looked like I was going to have to make a claim. I had it half in my head that I was packing in. I was out for that long.

"It was good to get back because everyone had written me off, even the managers and probably the board and everyone connected with the club. I was out for that long, so to come back and do what I did was brilliant for me."

But when Weaver did return to action after his long injury layoff, it was in bizarre circumstances. Stuart Pearce had just signed a deal to become the next boss with one game of the season remaining. City were in eighth position, while seventh would have been enough to qualify for the UEFA Cup.

Naturally, they were up against Middlesbrough – who were occupying that coveted European spot. A win for the Blues would have lifted them above their opponents, while the Teesiders needed just a draw to be playing on the continent the following season.

Weaver was on the bench for the game, with David James starting. The away side went 1-0 up through Jimmy Floyd Hasselbaink, but, right after half time, Kiki Musampa equalised for the hosts. That, though, wasn't enough and – in the 88th minute – Pearce unleashed his master plan.

To simplify the move, the tactic was 'aim for the big man'. It's just that the big man in question was his goalkeeper, David James – meaning Weaver came on to fill in between the sticks. How much did he know about the scheme?

"Nothing," he says, still with a sense of shock of what happened on his face. "I didn't have a clue. Didn't have a clue. And I asked Jamo afterwards and he said, 'Oh, yeah. I knew about the plan.' And Pearcey must have been sat at home thinking, 'What can we do if things aren't quite going right? Is there anything we can do to surprise them?'

"I remember being sat on the bench next to Jon Macken, and Tim Flowers [City's then goalkeeping coach], with about ten minutes left, said, 'Go and get warmed up.'"

He does a movement with his head as if he's looking over his shoulder, confused as to who Flowers could have been talking to.

"He said, 'You're going on in a minute. Weaves – you! Get warmed up!'"

Weaver's voice is now as high as it's been all interview.

"So I've gone for a run and then..." he makes a whistling noise and waves, as if he's being called in to get ready to be subbed on. "I'm thinking he can't just be putting me on for five minutes to say 'thanks for coming', that sort of thing.

"And then I saw the kitman, Chappy [Les Chapman], pull out an outfield shirt with number one, James on it. Next minute, I saw Jamo running over taking his top off and put his thing on. Claudio Reyna came off and I've gone on.

"It wasn't for two minutes, by the time injury time was up it was probably the best part of ten minutes. But Jamo was terrible, wasn't he? He caused a bit of havoc and we got the penalty – you'd have put your life on Robbie [Fowler] scoring it. Anyway, he didn't.

"That was my first action in a proper game for a few years and I remember getting a great reception off the fans when I came on. I remember after the game, I was sat down and the lads were in the dressing room with their heads in their hands and couldn't believe that we'd just missed out.

"But I was just sat there, trying to look a bit gutted, but I was buzzing inside that I'd got on. I remember doing a decent save from Stewart Downing and all summer I was just buzzing. I was disappointed we didn't get into Europe, but, really selfishly and personally, inside I was jumping for joy."

The Saturday before I travelled to meet with the ex-City keeper, Weaver had joined the action for his new club – Aberdeen – from the bench, after Jamie Langfield had been sent off for a foul on one of Weaver's old teammates, Georgios Samaras, now of Celtic.

His girlfriend had reminded him of that Middlesbrough match in 2005 after his latest appearance, because that City match was the first she'd been to: "I'd not been going out with her long," he says, "and she thought that happened all the time. She'd said, 'Oh, does that not normally happen then?' and I said, 'That'll probably never happen again in our lifetimes!'"

David James continued to be the club's number one for the following season, but as the 2006-07 campaign approached, Weaver thought his future was in jeopardy: "I remember going away to China and Joe Hart had just come. David James was still there. We got back from China and I walked in from training one day and I saw this big, skinny, gangly lad."

Suddenly Weaver's whispering to me: "And I'm thinking, 'I recognise him'. And then I've gone, 'That's that Swedish keeper! Fucking great! Jamo's still here – what am I going to do?!'

"He [Andreas Isaksson] signed, the next day Jamo went to Portsmouth and I thought he [Isaksson] was going to play. They'd just spent two and a half million on him, he'd just played every game in the World Cup, he had 40-odd caps for Sweden, so obviously he'd signed him to play to replace David James.

"We were playing Chelsea away on the first game. We trained Saturday morning and he got injured – I think he did his ankle. Stuart Pearce turned to me and said I was playing.

"We lost 3-0, but it was my first start for the club in about three and a half years or something. I felt I did ok in that game. I wasn't at fault for any of the goals and made a couple of decent saves and my distribution was ok. There's no shame in losing away at Chelsea; they were champions."

The following game saw Weaver's first clean sheet in the Premier League since his return. Portsmouth came to Eastlands and the game will probably be remembered more for a horrible challenge by Ben Thatcher on Pedro Mendes than the 0-0 scoreline.

But the fixture list hadn't exactly been kind to the Blues, given that next up was Arsenal at home. Weaver, though, was in good form and kept another clean sheet, saving several times from Thierry Henry, while Robin van Persie hit the post. At the other end, Joey Barton dispatched a penalty and the home side won 1-0.

"I was just enjoying playing," Weaver says, "and by this time Isaksson had got back fit so I was keeping him out of the team. Which was great for me, but I felt under a little bit of pressure because I was thinking that he [Stuart Pearce] had paid two and a bit million for him and was going to want to get him in, so if I make a slight error then he's going to put him in.

"Joe Hart played against Sheffield United at home because I tweaked my back. I was messing about after training and someone had a shot and I tweaked a muscle in my back. And then I clashed with Dunney [Richard Dunne] against Reading and had to come off, and I think Isaksson played the next game away at Portsmouth. But Pearcey put me straight back in.

"I was really pleased that he put me back in. But then we lost to Blackburn away in the quarter final of the FA Cup on a Sunday afternoon. We lost 2-0. I remember it now – Aaron Mokoena and Matt Derbyshire scored. And I never played again. I never knew walking off that pitch that day, that that was going to be my last game.

"We played on the Wednesday night against Chelsea. He put Isaksson in, there was about ten games to go and I never played again for City."

"We got back from China and I walked in from training one day and I saw this big, skinny, gangly lad. And I'm thinking, 'I recognise him'. And then I've gone, 'That's that Swedish keeper!'"

That summer saw huge changes at City. Stuart Pearce was sacked as the manager, while then-chairman John Wardle was searching for a buyer, eventually selling to the controversial Thaksin Shinawatra. Meanwhile, Weaver – who was out of contract – ended up moving on a Bosman to Charlton Athletic.

"I'd agreed a contract [at City]," Weaver says, when I ask whether he found the uncertainty difficult. "We started talking around Christmas time. I was playing so I felt I was in a reasonable position to ask for a new contract. We haggled, like you do – it's amazing, when you sign for a club it takes ten minutes, but when you're at a club, it takes six months. That's just how it is.

"We eventually got an agreement – a two year contract, with a testimonial – and I was all set to sign it, just after the season finished. We played Tottenham away on the last day and lost, and Stuart Pearce was sacked the next day.

"So my agent spoke to the chief exec and asked, 'What's happening with Nicky's contract? When are we going to come in and sign it?' As far as we were concerned, it was done. All the numbers were right and we'd done it.

"'We can't do anything yet. Obviously we've just sacked the manager, so give us a couple of days for everything to settle down...'

"'But Nicky's going away...'

"'As soon as he comes back off his holidays, come in and sign, no problem.'

"So I went away and came back and got straight onto my agent to find out what was happening.

"'Just give us a week, we're trying to sell the club – we can't really do anything as we speak, but as soon as the takeover happens, Nicky'll sign.'

"So I didn't think much of it. Time starts creeping on and we're getting into the middle of June and they're still saying, 'We want you to come in.' And I'm thinking, they've got no manager and they've not really got an owner.

"But it had been announced that I'd agreed a new deal, so I think everyone thought I'd signed a new deal. There was no real interest in me because we didn't canvas any and my agent wasn't ringing about. And then it got to a point where it was like, 'We might have to start having a look around here, because if they suddenly get a new manager, he might want to bring his own goalkeeper in.'

"The rumours then started that Sven Goran Eriksson was going to take over, so I'm thinking, 'Well, he's Swedish. He's going to go for the Swedish lad.' Which is a bit daft, really, but that's what I was thinking.

It's all well and good them saying they want me, but they've got no manager and no owner. I was desperate to stay. I did not want to leave.

"And then I was golfing in Scotland, right in the highlands of Scotland, and I barely got any phone reception up there. I went to a restaurant on the Saturday night and my agent – who was Paul Stretford, at the time – rang me up and said, 'Nicky, we're going to speak to Alan Pardew at Charlton on Wednesday.'

"And I said, 'But I don't want to go to Charlton.' And he said, 'Well, we're going to speak to him.'

"I went down on the Wednesday and Alan Pardew spoke to me. They'd just been relegated from the Premier League, they were the favourites to win the league, they were throwing a lot of money about and they'd made some big signings, there were some big transfer fees.

"He [Pardew] said to me, 'You're not leaving this ground today without making a decision.' I thought I'd go down, have a chat with them, come back and have a chat with City and have a week to think about it. He said, 'You've got a bit of time, but you are not leaving without a yes or a no.'

"...we'd agreed a deal and I was sort of happy with it. I didn't want to move to London, I didn't want to leave City, but I was thinking I was definitely going to be playing. I signed and it was the worst thing I ever did."

"Obviously he was trying to bully me into signing, but we'd agreed a deal and I was sort of happy with it. I didn't want to move to London, I didn't want to leave City, but I was thinking I was definitely going to be playing. I signed and it was the worst thing I ever did.

"In hindsight, I should have stayed because Isaksson got injured and Kasper [Schmeichel] ended up starting. So I'd have thought I'd have definitely started.

"I'll always be grateful to City because of the knee thing and sending me to America and giving me a platform. I had ten years there, which was fantastic, but the only thing I got was a text off John Wardle, who was outgoing chairman. And I think someone had said, 'You've got to speak to Nicky.'

"I was disappointed with how it was all done, but it doesn't mar anything."

After leaving Charlton in 2009, Weaver joined Dundee United and played every game until his contract expired five months later. He then moved to Burnley for the remainder of the season, but didn't make an appearance for the club.

From there, he re-joined his boyhood club Sheffield Wednesday, where he, once again, became a penalty shootout hero. It was the Johnstone's Paint Trophy second round and the Owls faced Chesterfield at Hillsborough.

"We got to the penalties and just kept taking them," he says. "I remember saving three – two of them in sudden death, so if they'd have scored we'd have gone out. And it never ever dawned on me that it was going to come around to me.

"I wasn't counting the penalties, obviously I'm not with the lads in the middle. For a penalty, I go in, they either score or miss, and I walk to the side and that's what we do. We don't really look at the lads or anything.

"I've saved a penalty, I think. And then I've walked to the side. And the linesman's gone, 'It's you.' I looked round and all the lads on the halfway line are pointing me back in. And I thought, 'Oh, bollocks, I've got to take one here, what am I going to do?' I never even thought about taking one.

"So I thought, 'Right, just put it in the corner. Sidefoot and in the corner.' And then I thought, 'No. Just take a goal kick, but keep your head down and it should stay low.'

"I thought I've got to just belt it," he laughs. "The run up was massive. And I've kept my head down and just pinged it straight into the roof of the net down the middle. Then it was their goalie's turn and he tried to go for the top corner and missed it.

"I'd stood on that Kop as a kid for years, and to save three penalties in front of it and to score was amazing. It was only a Johnstone's Paint game, but I never thought I'd score in front of the Kop that I used to stand on for years."

In 2012, though, Chris Kirkland signed for the Owls and replaced Weaver as the club's first choice. In July 2013, he moved back up to Scotland once again, having been released by Wednesday at the end of his contract.

"Derek McInnes rang me and he'd tried to sign me before when he was manager of St Johnstone and I really fancied it," he says. "It's something different, the SPL is a good platform and, no disrespect to League One and League Two, but I didn't want to dog around the lower divisions. I've got no qualms about doing it in the future, but Aberdeen's a big club and a big city and I just fancied it.

"I spoke to them for a couple of weeks and they were really keen to get it done. And after a little bit, the phone wasn't ringing and I'd already made my mind up. I knew a couple of the lads there – Willo Flood, actually, who was at City, I'd always kept in touch with him. And he was ringing me every half an hour saying, 'Get yourself up here, the gaffer's had a word with me, it's great,' that sort of thing.

"But it's a great club and I'm 34 now and at 24 I thought I was done. I've played nearly 400 games now and, to be still playing at 34, I feel really lucky.

"Obviously, when I started at City, everyone was saying, 'You're going to be the next England goalkeeper,' all that sort of stuff. In hindsight, I wouldn't have anticipated myself at 34 being here. But that's where I am and I've had a great career – probably not the career everyone thought I was going to have at 21.

"I was unlucky to get the injury, but lucky because you look at people like Paul Lake who had to pack in at 21 or 22 and who knows what might have happened.

"I want to play on for a few years and I just want to enjoy it now."

2 LEE CROOKS

Of the Manchester City team that played in the 1999 Division Two Play-Off Final, it's perhaps fullback Lee Crooks whose career took one of the most drastic turns. After finishing his playing days, he made the switch to the armed forces, becoming a gunner in the RAF. When I spoke to him near his home city of Wakefield, he was waiting for an operation on his neck before he could return to active service.

His football career began at City. He joined the youth setup and signed his first professional contract with the club in August 1994, aged 16. However, his years with the Blues probably suffered due to the unstable and turbulent nature of the club at the time.

CITY CAREER STATS

Apps: 90 (26 sub)
Goals: 2

Signed: August 1994
Left: March 2001

Debut: Port Vale (a), 1996
Result: 2-0 victory

"It was great," he says, looking back at his time at Maine Road, "I enjoyed it. There were some good coaches there as I was coming through. Colin Bell was my coach at the time and he played a big part in me coming over and into the setup. There was Neil McNab, too... they were all City old boys.

"As soon as I joined I knew that it was the club I wanted to be at. It was very family-orientated and I just loved it there. There was never a decision that needed to be made, I wanted to be at City."

By 1996, Crooks was regularly being involved in the matchday squad and he made his debut for the first team in the September of that year. City were travelling away to Port Vale, a game that the Blues went on to win 2-0 with goals from Uwe Rosler and Paul Dickov.

I ask him if he remembers it. "Not really, no," he replies, before going on to remember it exactly. "I think one of the games – Phil Neal might have been manager – I came on as a sub at Port Vale. It was a very bleak night, but it was a dream come true for me. I was a young lad and just being told I was in the squad for one game was unbelievable, but then getting on that night was the best feeling ever.

"There were a lot of ups and downs and different managers and things with the chairman that were going on," he says, "but there were a lot of good characters in the first team dressing room. There were the likes of Niall Quinn and Tony Coton, but they were down to earth. I looked up to them, but they had their feet on the ground. They always wanted a bit of banter with you, but you could talk to them."

For Crooks, coming through the ranks was a completely different experience to how professional footballers progress now. In the modern game, youngsters' careers are modelled solely on their playing ability, while in years gone by, youth team players were expected to do the chores around the club to earn respect and take responsibility. It's a system that Crooks seems to value and he's not convinced things have changed for the better.

"We all had our jobs to do," he says of his time as a youth player, "we'd be cleaning the boots and stuff like that. It was a good environment and a very homely environment. Every day was a privilege to get up and go to work. That was my job and what more could a young lad want?"

One of the biggest problems Crooks faced in breaking into the first team squad was the size of the playing staff at that time. There have been reports of up to 50 senior professionals on the club's books, with manager Joe Royle later commenting that there were international players who couldn't get a game with the reserves because of the competition they faced.

"The coaches that were around had faith in the young lads," he says, "there was me, Michael Brown, Chris Greenacre, Jeff Whitley, these kinds of lads, and they always used to tell us to keep our heads down and we'll get our chance. I got my chance, so I think it was just down to the manager, really.

"Even when we did get in to training with the first team down at Platt Lane, that was an honour," he continues. "The first team lads were always there to help you and always kept your feet on the ground. It

"The first team lads were always there to help you and keep your feet on the ground. It was a bit surreal, though, because you'd be training with them, but then you'd have to go back to doing your jobs. So we'd be back over at Maine Road washing the floors and scrubbing the boots!"

was a bit surreal, though, because you'd be training with them, but then you'd have to go back to doing your jobs. So we'd be back over at Maine Road washing the floors and scrubbing the boots!"

Having broken into the team at City, did Crooks ever feel any extra pressure to perform because of the club's struggles in Division One? In his first season in the main squad, the Blues finished 14th in the league, while in his second they were relegated.

"I think, as a young lad, when you get into the team – and obviously Maine Road was always packed, there was always 28 or 30 thousand people there, no matter what division we were in and we always had a lot of support – and things are going against you and you're down there and struggling, it's down to you, really. It's up to you and the players around you to focus on the job in hand.

"I didn't get too involved in that, I just went out there and played football. I just tried to concentrate on my job and kicking the ball about – I wasn't good at anything else. I wasn't really that good at football, like!

"It's just concentration and it was a privilege to play for such a big team even though they were hard times. I look back now and they were great times, really."

Midway through Crooks' second season in the first team, there was another change of manager. This time, though, the new man was to last a lot longer than some of his predecessors, as Joe Royle came in to try and save the club from relegation. As we now know, he wasn't quite able to put the brakes on the slide down the table in time, but he would – over the course of the next three years – get the Blues in forward gear.

"Joe was fantastic," Crooks says. "Before I came to City I was at Oldham Athletic as a young lad and Joe and Willie [Donachie] were coaches there. So I'd worked with him as a young lad and he was very much into the youth system at Oldham. He was always with the youngsters, so when he came from Everton into City, I was over the moon.

"Both Joe and Willie helped me a lot as a young lad when I was growing up and with keeping my feet on the ground, so it was fantastic.

"He'd always tell you whether you were right or wrong and he wasn't afraid to set you straight," he continues. "If you weren't in the team, he'd tell you why you weren't in the team, he wouldn't just leave you hanging all the time. You knew where you stood with him, so I respected him. He was a fantastic manager and a great bloke as well.

"And it was the same for Willie, he was outstanding. He was another one who you could just go up to and talk to as a young lad and he'd work with you and help you."

When the Blues were relegated to Division Two, Crooks says he was expecting a tough time. The club had underachieved for several seasons running and the fans that had been travelling to Premier League away grounds two years earlier would now be going to watch their team play in the third tier of English football.

"Being such a big club like Manchester City and being relegated again wasn't good news, so we knew the pressure was going to be on," he says. "Every time we had teams coming to Maine Road like it was an FA Cup Final for them. More or less their gameplan was always to keep us quiet for 20 minutes, hope the crowd would get on our backs, and then hope it'd become a mess for us.

"It was a hard season down in Division Two, definitely," he continues, "especially in that first half of the season when we were really struggling. We started hitting a bit of form just before Christmas – maybe at the right time. I remember playing Wrexham away and we started picking up points and the lads started believing in themselves.

"As a footballer, it's a long season anyway. There are a lot of games, there are cup games, and playing down in Division Two there's a lot of rough and tumble. It's different football altogether. Our main aim was to be promoted automatically, but the way things were going [at the start], we'd have been happy

"Every time we had teams coming to Maine Road like it was an FA Cup Final for them. More or less their gameplan was always to keep us quiet for 20 minutes, hope the crowd would get on our backs, and then hope it'd become a mess for us."

getting into the play-offs. We probably just about hit form at the right time to get there, really, so it worked out well for us."

Playing as a fullback, Crooks wasn't the most prolific of scorers – what fullbacks ever are, really? – but it was during the 1998-99 season that the defender got his name on the scoresheet for the first time. At the end of February, the Blues travelled to Chesterfield and found themselves behind thanks to a first half strike from David Reeves.

"We went to three at the back," Crooks remembers, "I can remember Joe telling me to go to the left hand side to play three at the back. I got the ball – I can't remember who passed it to me – and I was running down the left. All I could hear was the gaffer absolutely hammering me: 'Pass the fucking ball! Pass the ball!'

"Anyway, I came inside and just gave it a whack. I just hit it and fortunately it went in. After the game, I went into the changing rooms and the first thing Joe said to me was, 'It's a good job that went in, Crooksy, or you'd have been getting it now.' They were good times, but... I think it might have been a cross to be fair!"

Preparations for the play-offs were able to begin before the end of the season. A draw and a defeat in the final three games meant that the club were sure to be finishing no higher than third before kick-off on the final day. It had the added bonus that, by the time the first semi-final with Wigan came around, the squad had had chance to get ready.

"We just carried [our form] on," Crooks says, "Joe took us away and we trained on Maine Road for a bit. Confidence was high in the camp and we just had to try and get the two games out of the way. Obviously, Wigan being a local derby was a big game as well.

"I remember going to Wigan and going 1-0 down more or less straight away. I'd not even touched the ball and we were a goal behind. So I was thinking, 'Oh, here we go!' But I suppose it's just City, never doing things the easy way, it's always the hard way."

Following the semi-final victory, the Blues set a date with Gillingham at Wembley. Crooks was just 21 years old for what would turn out to be one of the most important games in the club's history.

"I was rooming with Weaves [Nicky Weaver]," he says, "and we always used to have a chicken club sandwich the night before and a drink of blackcurrant and lemonade and all that lot. We went for a walk around London and it was a bit surreal. The City fans were well up for it. London was packed with them as we were walking down the street.

"Then we went back to the room and had a bit of a talk with the gaffer. We got our suits on and then we were on our way to Wembley – coming up Wembley Way on the coach showed the nature of the game and how important it was to the club at the time. That really hit home because it was just a sea of blue shirts. The coach was moving so slowly into the stadium because of all the fans that that's when it really hit me that we needed to do it."

For a player who'd only recently broken into the team from the academy set-up, was Crooks nervous before the match?

He thinks about his answer for a while, before saying he wasn't: "More excited, I think," he replies, "once I'd been out and warmed up, I was more excited. Especially at the old Wembley, the tunnel was behind the goal and it was really long, too.

"Going back inside and getting ready, and then the teams coming out, that's when it got a bit real," he continues, "I remember coming out of the tunnel because it was like someone hiking the volume up on a hi-fi. The closer we got, the scream and the roar was unbelievable, with the fireworks, too. Just talking about it makes the hairs on the back of my neck stand up."

Crooks' game ended on 85 minutes, with the Blues 1-0 down. With just five minutes of time remaining, the manager brought on Gareth Taylor and went to a back three in an attempt to add more firepower to draw level.

"I remember the pitch was absolutely soaking wet," Crooks says, "I must have fallen on my backside about three or four times inside the first ten minutes. I remember that because the gaffer was caning me: 'Have you got studs on?!'

"We had a couple of chances," he remembers, "I must have gone close with a shot from about 25 or 30 yards out that went just past the post, but with Gillingham it was always going to be a hard game anyway. They were a tough team. They had Bob Taylor up front, Carl Asaba too. They were strong lads and good finishers – they scored plenty of goals between them.

"They also had Andy Hessenthaler in midfield, who must be about 60 now and only just retired! He was a fit and strong lad, so it was a really hard game for us. Obviously going 2-0 down wasn't what we'd hoped for!

"Though, even when it went to 2-0, because they'd got so deep, we always knew there was going to be a chance," he says. "We believed there was a chance, I don't know if anyone else did. Obviously some people in the crowd didn't because some went home! Thankfully, Kev [Horlock] and Dicky [Paul Dickov] popped up and it was all back on."

"I remember the pitch was soaking wet. I must have fallen on my backside about three or four times inside the first ten minutes. I remember that because the gaffer was caning me: 'Have you got studs on?!'"

With Crooks off the pitch and unable to do anything but watch as Gillingham scored their second, how was he feeling? Was it – somehow – worse for him to have to sit on the bench and just hope that the players on the field could turn it around?

"Not really," he says, looking back, "I think I was dead on my feet, to be honest. It was hard and at 2-0 down, Joe's got to go for it. Big Gaz Taylor came on, which is what you need when you're in that position. I knew when I came off the pitch, I'd given everything I had. I was out on my feet, it had been a long season and Wembley's an unforgiving place – it's a big old pitch, it was wet as well, so it was really heavy.

"You've just got to have faith in the lads and I think that's one thing we did have. We all had faith in each other. We were all friends on and off the pitch and I think that showed at the time. I don't think we were amazing players, but we were good mates. It didn't matter if you were dropped or you were sub, we all wanted the right things for each other and we all cared for each other and that showed in the end."

One of the recurring themes throughout this book will be the team spirit that Manchester City side had. Each of the players remembers it very fondly and Crooks is no different: "It was fantastic. From the more experienced players like Ian Bishop or Kev Horlock or Dicky to the young lads like Edgy [Richard Edghill] or Weaves – who went on to have a great career at City. To have those kinds of lads around us was fantastic.

"It meant a lot to us and I think we were all very grounded people," he continues, "if anyone had a problem, the lads would help them out. If you were taken out of the team, there was none of this 'I want to leave' and all this kind of stuff. You

"I've only been back to the Etihad once or twice and how far the club has come is a credit to them. It's good to see that all the fans and supporters who stuck by us through those years are getting it all back now."

stood by what the gaffer said and you wanted the best for the team. It was successful and that's why we were successful.

"I think most of the lads would admit we weren't the greatest of players, but what we did was to try and work for each other and that showed."

The game at Wembley still sits as one of Crooks' proudest achievements in his career. "It's a massive part of me," he says, "I'm so proud of starting there as a kid and coming through the ranks, that's everything to a young lad. I'm just glad I was part of that, especially looking at where the club is now.

"I've only been back to the Etihad once or twice and how far the club has come is a credit to them. It's good to see that all the fans and supporters who stuck by us through those years are getting it all back now. It's always been a fantastic club and the support that they have, home and away, is brilliant.

"I've been on the other side of the world – I was in Afghanistan – and people would come up to me and say, 'I was at that game, Gillingham vs. Man City, it was amazing, wasn't it?'

"That's just a game that the City fans who were there will never forget. They've had a lot of success recently, but that game goes down as a bit of history."

When Crooks' playing days finished, his career took a drastic turn. After retiring from football, he enlisted in the armed forces, eventually becoming a gunner in the RAF.

"I wanted away from football, I just totally wanted to get away from it," he says. "If I'd never been a footballer, I'd always wanted to go into the forces. My brother served and so I thought I should give it a go. I spoke to my brother about it and he encouraged me. I was still fit enough.

"So I tried my luck at it and got through all my selections," he continues, "then that was it. It's been another part of my life and a huge experience that's opened my eyes up.

"I think it makes it all the better with what's happened in my career before because it made me realise how lucky I was. It's easy to think, 'Oh, I'm a footballer' and you don't realise how lucky you are – even lads these days have everything they need. They've got their health and they're getting paid for something they love doing.

"It's a gift, but it should be an honour. I see players moaning, but then I realise how the forces has put it all into perspective for me. It's made me a better person, really."

It's been quite a career change for the former footballer. He's now a regiment gunner, which means he's an infantry soldier. But Crooks says there's not a huge difference between how he approached his

"There's quite a few City fans on my squadron. When I came on to the squadron they were all there with their City shirts on and saying, 'I was there at Wembley' or they'd been to this game or that game..."

life as a footballer and now his life as a soldier: "Just like football, a lot of training and dedication goes into getting ready to go on operations.

"We can be training for eight to twelve months to go on one operation. So it's just the same as football, really – you train all week for a match on the Saturday, but our matchdays are just in a foreign country at the moment.

"For every person in the forces, it's all based on teamwork, too," he continues. "The guys that are out there serving now, from cooks to the fighter jet pilots to the infantry soldiers, we're all one big team. If one cog of that doesn't work, then none of it will. It's a massive team game and you need lads at the side of you who you can put your trust in."

Crooks' career in the RAF has seen him in combat in Afghanistan – an atmosphere that's much removed to the one of walking out onto the Wembley turf as a 21-year-old fullback.

"Even though you are going away with a lot of lads, it's a very lonely place," he says, "it's very eerie. It's very lonely being away from your family – that's a big one. It's a brutal environment and it really hits home what's going on in the world.

"It makes you not take things for granted – things like water or heating or getting fed every day. We've got great hospitals... we've got everything, but we still seem to moan about it. I don't see reason to moan about it, we've got everything we need.

"It was a life-changing experience for me," he says, "but for the better. In a crazy way, after it had settled a bit, I kind of enjoyed it."

While out in Afghanistan, Crooks wasn't short of attention from his fellow soldiers because of his past career as a footballer. "There's quite a few City fans on my squadron," he says, "when I came on to the squadron they were all there with their City shirts on and saying, 'I was there at Wembley' or they'd been to this game or that game.

"All the Manchester lads on my squadron are Blues. They're always asking me questions and stuff like that. Or it's, 'Can you get me this?' or, 'Can you get me that?', but I've not been back to the club for years!

"We have a kick about out in the desert," he continues, "yeah, it's alright."

3 RICHARD EDGHILL

Having seen the team come from two goals down and equalise in normal time, and having gone through the agony of being unable to break Gillingham down in extra time, the City fans that had travelled to Wembley were in for a shock in the penalty shootout. With the contest finely balanced at 2-1 – following successful spot-kicks from Kevin Horlock and Terry Cooke for the Blues, and John Hodge for the Gils – there was immense pressure on City's fourth taker. A miss would have let their opponents right back into the game, while a conversion meant any mistake from the next Gillingham taker would end the tie.

Without ever having scored a goal for the club, supporters were shocked to see Richard Edghill jogging forward. City hearts were in mouths as he placed the ball down on the spot and stepped back to begin his run up. But all the fears were quickly washed away, as the defender netted one of the best penalties of the season: a placed a side-footed strike into Vince Bartram's top left corner via the underside of the crossbar, sending the Gillingham keeper the wrong way in the process.

The celebration was of a man who didn't score many, too – as he waved his arms around, pumped his fists and then kissed the club's crest on his shirt. The embarrassment aside, it was clearly a feeling echoed by the City fans behind the goal and, in the end, it turned out to be the winning spot-kick.

CITY CAREER STATS

Apps: 210 (4 sub)
Goals: 1

Signed: July 1992
Left: July 2002

Debut: Wimbledon (a), 1993
Result: 1-0 defeat

"We'd practised penalties every day in training in between the Wigan game and the Play-Off Final," the former fullback says, "every day, a few of the lads would stay behind and practise against Weaves [Nicky Weaver] and big Tommy Wright and I think we'd sort of decided who'd take them that week.

"Joe [Royle] just came up to me and asked if I'd be willing to take one," he says, talking about the end of extra time at Wembley. "I said yes because I had the confidence from not missing too many in training. I'd always gone the same way and the keeper just never seemed to save them. So I knew that, if it went to penalties, I'd be taking one. It was only after the extra time had finished that it dawned on me and I

"I remember being stood in the tunnel and having Vinnie Jones, John Fashanu, and a load of other tough players stood there and I was thinking, 'Have I done the right thing here?'"

thought, 'Shit, I'm actually going to have to stand up and take one now!'

"I didn't mean to go that close to the bar," he adds, "I'd practised the same way every time and I'd always gone roughly to the middle of the goal. I think nerves played a big part in it. I think I put the ball down and stepped back and felt really nervous. Luckily, it went in."

It was the first time Edghill had been responsible for sending the ball into the net for City, despite having played for the Blues since 1993, some five seasons earlier. It wouldn't go down as his first goal for the club, given it was in a penalty shootout, though the fullback doesn't seem to mind: "I think I scored the season after against Blackburn at home," he says. "I used to get a lot of stick from people for not scoring a lot of goals, but I was an out-and-out defender. I loved defending, that's how I'd grown up and, for me, that was the most important thing."

Born in Oldham, Edghill began his professional career coming through the ranks at City. He joined the Centre of Excellence aged 12, where he would do weekly training sessions every Thursday at Platt Lane. "It was only for two hours after school," he says. "They used to be taken by a guy called George Smith and then later it was Colin Bell.

"It was exciting because I'd had the chance to go to a couple of different clubs," he continues. "Scouts used to come regularly to watch our games too, but it was that progression from playing Sunday League football to going into a professional environment. I didn't really think I had much of a chance, but I really enjoyed it when I was there."

From joining the youth setup in 1988, Edghill progressed to the first team at the start of the 1993-94 season. "I made my debut on a Monday evening against Wimbledon," he says, "I remember being stood in the tunnel and having Vinnie Jones, John Fashanu, and a load of other tough players stood there and I was thinking, 'Have I done the right thing here?' But I went on to enjoy the game."

Despite the worries of facing tough opposition players, Edghill quickly developed a reputation as a defender with something of a hefty tackle himself. He says that this is one area where he feels the game has changed: "Back when I was playing, you could get away with kicking somebody. Nowadays, you can't do it because there are TV cameras everywhere. I used to enjoy getting stuck in and that was part and parcel of the game."

It's hard to ignore one of the fiercest tackles the defender ever made when asking him about how the game's changed. In October 1994, the Blues travelled to Loftus Road to take on a QPR side that had won just one of their first nine Premier League games. They had one of the best chances they could have asked for to make it two from ten when City arrived, as the visiting side ended up have two players dismissed – first, goalkeeper Andy Dibble saw red for a two-footed challenge on Les Ferdinand, then Edghill picked up a second yellow for a robust tackle on Trevor Sinclair.

"I got sent off in the second half for a nothing challenge in my eyes, but I think the first tackle in the first half was worse, when I was shown a yellow card," he says, "thinking back now, I should definitely have had a red. As he [Sinclair] got the ball and turned, I just dived in, about knee-high. If I did that challenge these days, I'd easily have got a four or five game ban."

Having forced his way into the fold, though, the defender suffered a serious knee injury that would hamper his progress, following a series of fitness issues that saw him in and out of the team. "It was frustrating because I seemed to get a good run and then I'd get an injury," he says, "and then the knee injury came along at Leeds, which kept me out for 22 months. I seemed to be on the sidelines forever, watching the team and the club at the time going downhill. It was more frustrating because I just wanted to play.

"I always think back to certain stages that I went through," he continues, "I remember the day it happened and I remember thinking it wasn't a bad one. That was until I stood up and realised my foot was facing the wrong way. Then I sat back down and realised how bad it was.

"I didn't really have a lot of swelling. I got to the dressing room and they packed my knee with ice and the next thing I remember was waking up in the hospital in Whalley Range, with my knee absolutely huge after an operation.

"I'd had quite a few different operations, from having a camera inserted to have a look at the damage, to the main operation to correct the problem, but I think it was probably about eight months down the line was when I was starting to have doubts as to whether I'd ever play again.

"It was such a long journey to get fit again that I never thought I'd do it," he continues. "I had a lot of help from Paul Lake with the rehabilitation. If it wasn't for him and for Mandy and Phillipa at the Beaumont Hospital, I don't think I'd have got back."

When Edghill did get back into contention for the first team, matters on the pitch had gone from bad to worse. The club had been relegated from the Premier League and were in the midst of a relegation battle to stay in Division One – a battle they would go on to lose.

"The preseason we did [for 1998-99] was a tough one," he says, "but I remember running out against Blackpool on the opening day and we had 32,000 fans inside Maine Road for the old Third Division. I think, as a team, we went into that season expecting to demolish teams and we won that first game quite comfortably. But then the reality kicked in and we realised it wasn't going to be that easy.

"We were getting a lot of stick as well," he continues, as he talks about a difficult start to the campaign, "we weren't beating teams as comfortably as the fans would have liked, so it was difficult to take. We just wanted to get on a good run and I think we started to do that after a game on Boxing Day, away at Wrexham.

"I remember sitting in the dressing room after the game and Kevin Horlock sat next to me and said, 'I think that's probably the worst performance I've ever seen by any professional player.' And I did have a bad game..."

"It was a scruffy 1-0 win. It was windy, it was rainy, the pitch wasn't great, but the away fans that day – our fans – were amazing and we got a bit lucky. I remember sitting in the dressing room after the game and Kevin Horlock sat next to me and said, 'I think that's probably the worst performance I've ever seen by any professional player.' And I did have a bad game, but then the lads sat there and we realised we might have a chance of automatic promotion.

"But, as we went on and as the games were counting down, it became obvious we were going to be in the play-offs," he says. "By then, though, we had that fantastic team spirit that had built up."

The season culminated with the play-offs, starting with two semi-finals against Wigan. The first match, at Springfield Park, was a blur for Edghill, who explains that his only real memory is of an incident in the tunnel at half time: "Andy Morrison and Eric Nixon had a fight," he says, "we'd gone 1-0 down really early on and we'd come in at half time and I just remember this almighty kerfuffle.

"Eric Nixon and Andy Morrison were going blow for blow and people were getting thrown all over the place. Police and stewards had to come in to separate them."

After pulling it back to 1-1 at Springfield Park, the Blues went on to ease past Wigan 1-0 at Maine Road to set themselves up with a trip to Wembley. "The atmosphere totally changed," Edghill says, "everyone was really excited to get into training and the training was lively, with a lot of confidence around. It was a good place to be.

"We trained on Maine Road most days and we all ate together after training. Joe [Royle] and Willie [Donachie] brought that in and I think that was what caused us to have a good team spirit. That's what got us through it all."

The team stayed together the night before the big game and Edghill remembers how he felt when he woke up the following morning vividly: "I looked out of the window and I could see the towers at Wembley," he says, "I don't remember the hotel, but that's when the nerves started to kick in.

"On the coach, I always used to sit in the same seat for away games," he continues, "there were just blue shirts and the yellow and dark shirts that we used to play in – the away kit that we wore that day. I'd never seen so many fans on one street as there were on Wembley Way. That's stuck with me ever since.

"I think it did [put pressure on the team] because I think it was then that I realised that it was real. We'd obviously thought about it a lot, but seeing that made it real.

"As for the game, people always ask me if I remember this incident or if I remember that and I have to say no," Edghill says, "I remember early on that I had a diving header at the far post – and it was very rare for me to get that far up the pitch! It went wide.

"I remember the pitch being huge. I always thought Maine Road was big, but Wembley was probably the biggest pitch I've played on. It was quite soft and I didn't think I was going to last the 90 minutes."

It was here that I asked Edghill about Gillingham's goals. The second – which made it 2-0 – came with just three minutes to play, so I asked the fullback what went through his head when Robert Taylor hit the back of Nicky Weaver's net.

He laughs, then asks me: "Am I allowed to swear?

"Straight away, I thought about the following season," he says. "I was beginning to wonder if I could take another season in Division Two, because I think it took its toll on a lot of the lads, mentality-wise. Then there were thoughts about having to go back to places like York – that just flashed through my head – and playing in poor stadiums, with bad pitches.

"Teams probably used to dig up the pitch the day before we were due to play them," he continues, "when we went to York I remember it was like it was worse than a Sunday League pitch. It was full of sand, it was wet, and it was like a bog.

"As soon as that goal went in, I was thinking, 'Not another season in this division' and when Kevin Horlock pulled one back I just felt a bit of relief that we had scored. I did think it was going to be a consolation because I didn't know if we had the time or energy to get another one.

"In that period between Kev scoring and Paul [Dickov] scoring, I think we'd had a few chances. We had to pile on the pressure and it was Last Chance Saloon almost, so for him to nip in with the equaliser the way he did was an unbelievable feeling."

Following on from that success on the pitch, Edghill's City career went from strength to strength. The next season, in which the Blues won automatic promotion back to the Premier League, the defender found himself as skipper for most of the campaign, following an injury to club captain Andy Morrison.

"I think Joe gave me the captaincy because I was one of the longest serving players," he says, "for me it was an honour to do it and I enjoyed it. I wasn't one of those captains who went around shouting and screaming at players – I just got on with my job and tried to do my best in training every day. I just tried to give 100 per cent all the time."

Having just come up from Division Two, the team continued to perform and carried on their good run of form from the year before. "There were some good teams in that division so I, personally, would have been looking for a mid-table finish.

"But we had that team spirit and that just carried us through," he continues, "for us to be where we were when we were, I think we did really well and put some good results together. We worked hard as a team; we weren't a team of fantastic players but we looked an organised, fit team."

For Edghill and the rest of the side that had played in the Gillingham game in 1999, May 2000 represented a bit of déjà vu. With the fixture computer sending the Blues to Ewood Park on the final day of the season, they needed a draw to be sure of automatic promotion.

Typically, Ipswich – in third place and two points behind City – were winning against Walsall at Portman Road, while the Blues went in a half time 1-0 down, thanks to a Matt Jansen strike.

"I think I was more excited about the Blackburn game than I was about the Play-Off Final, which was strange," Edghill says. "I remember driving to the stadium – I couldn't wait to get there, get into the changing rooms, get the kit on, and warm up.

"They had a few chances as well," he continues, "I think they hit the crossbar and the post about four or five times. To go 1-0 down and rely on other results was a blow, but we had that togetherness that I keep talking about. It happened quite a lot that season where we'd take a bit of a knock, but come back with goals.

"Paul Dickov was on fire that season again. Shaun Goater would score with the badge on his shirt – he'd score with every part of his body. Those two were great for us because they'd work their socks off and they wanted to win."

Both Dickov and Goater scored on that day at Ewood Park to help the Blues to an unlikely 4-1 victory. The result confirmed that City would join Charlton in the Premier League for the 2000-01 season, but it wasn't a campaign that Edghill would have particularly enjoyed.

When I ask what he remembers of that year, he takes a long moment to think about his answer. "It was different," he says, "obviously, we've gone up and there was a bit more media attention on us as a club. More money started coming into it and I think things started changing around the club; we were spending millions on players, bringing foreign players in, and that team spirit got a little bit lost.

"We didn't start that well," he continues, "we had a good win against Sunderland and then there was the Coventry game where I scored an own goal. The season just didn't go as well as I thought it would, for the club, for the team and for myself."

The defender struggled to deal with Craig Bellamy that August afternoon, as the pacey striker tested him throughout the first half – with Edghill offered little support from his teammates, too. 23 minutes into the match, a cross from John Eustace was flicked past Nicky Weaver – who had come to deal with it, but didn't appear to have shouted for it – by the fullback.

The second goal came through Bellamy, too: he drove to the byline as Edghill did his best to show him wide when left one-on-one with the Welshman, but managed to force his shot past Weaver at his near post.

On 50 minutes, manager Joe Royle chose to substitute the defender and he was booed off the pitch by sections of the City crowd when Tony Grant came on to replace him. Edghill didn't feature again for the Blues for just over four months.

"I was frustrated," Edghill says of that substitution, "Joe had come in and I was upset about the boos I was getting. Looking back at the goals, I don't think there's much more I could have done. I've done that header for the own goal hundreds of times in training and in games, so it wasn't a freak thing. Normally, the goalkeeper gives a shout or he knows what I'm going to do and he stands his ground. For some reason, Weaves moved to the side of the goal.

"And the second one," he continues, "I think was a breakaway. I think we had a corner and I was the last man – I always stayed back at corners. I ended up one-on-one and just tried to guide him [Bellamy] away from the goal, which I did. He beat the goalkeeper on the near post and I got the stick for again – which I didn't understand.

"I was frustrated when Joe took me off and then he left me out of the next game. And then I didn't feature again until New Year's Day."

There was a sense of irony in Edghill's return to the team. He played three games on a loan spell at Birmingham before returning to City's starting line-up for the reverse fixture with Coventry.

"I think he [Joe Royle] had left me out and not given me an explanation so I got it into my head that I was going to get my head down, work hard and train well – just to carry on like I'd done throughout my career at the club. Then I got a call at home after I'd just got back in from taking my dogs for a walk and I was told to get ready to play against Coventry."

Despite the difficult campaign for Edghill, he bore no grudges and says he was "gutted" when he heard that Royle had been sacked that May. "I got on really well with Joe," he says, "he left me out of the team for most of that season, but I never fell out with him. I still spoke to him every day and I was gutted for him and Willie – they did really well for the club and had a good way of doing things.

"I felt players came in that I didn't think fitted that team

"I'd played under Kevin [Keegan] for the [England] Under-21s. He came in and said that all those players who'd been left out would start with a clean slate. And I thought, 'Yeah, I sort of half believe you, but we'll wait and see...'"

spirit we had," he continues. "I think there were more players coming in who thought they could just go out for a drink, or do this, or do that – and that changed the situation. There was a divide in the dressing room."

The change of manager possibly came at the wrong time for Edghill, too. Entering the final year of his contract, he also had to impress a new boss in order to earn an extension. In the end, it would turn out to be the defender's final year with the club.

"Bernard Halford had handed me a letter on the morning of the game [with West Brom]. I thought it was strange so I went downstairs and opened it and it was a contract offer of a year. And it said on it, 'You have seven days in which to reply to this letter' and I thought 'Why am I being given a timeframe to sign a contract?'"

"I'd played under Kevin [Keegan] for the [England] Under-21s," Edghill says. "He came in and said that all those players who'd been left out would start with a clean slate. And I thought, 'Yeah, I sort of half believe you, but we'll wait and see what happens.'

"So I just knuckled down and got on with it. I got myself fit and did everything that was asked of me and he changed the formation to wingbacks and 3-5-2, and I really enjoyed playing that position.

"I think I played up until the game with Sheffield Wednesday [on the 22 September]," he continues, "but then I damaged my medial ligament in my knee. I think Dennis Tueart was quoted after the Burnley game in the newspaper as saying that just because I'd played a few good games didn't mean I was going to get a new contract. I found it strange that our chief executive was saying that sort of thing in the paper.

"The issue of my contract came up around Boxing Day – Bernard Halford [the club secretary] had handed me a letter on the morning of the game [with West Brom]. I thought it was strange, so I went downstairs and opened it and it was a contract offer of a year. And it said on it, 'You have seven days in which to reply to this letter' and I thought, 'Why am I being given a timeframe to sign a contract?'

"And then that game I was sent off – I got two bookings – which added insult to injury," he says. He describes the red card, which replays later showed had been an incorrect decision: "I'd gone through and been brought down and it was shown to be a penalty. I was booked for diving – I've never been known for diving and I never have dived, so it was strange."

After the game, Edghill says he didn't do anything about the contract offer: "I was called into the office and Kevin Keegan said to me, 'You have a contract offer on the table and if you don't sign it, you won't be getting another one.'

"So that was when I knew I would be leaving," he continues, "he totally changed towards me. He decided he was going to make me train with the kids and the youth team. A few of the other lads, like Kevin Horlock, were taking the mickey out of me every day – which hurt a lot. I'd been with the club since I was 12 and to be told I was training with the youth team, it did hurt. I decided I wasn't going to stay and that's how it finished.

"Towards the end, it changed because I wouldn't sign a one-year contract on a lot less money than some of the players – some were getting four or five times what I was being offered. For me, it wasn't about the money. I was 27, I was probably coming into my prime, I'd got over my knee injury – I was more unhappy with the length of the contract.

"And then there was the issue of a testimonial. If I'd got a contract longer than one year, I'd probably have got a testimonial from the club, but then he [Keegan] quashed that and said they club weren't doing them any more. He then told me, 'You think this club owes you something.'

"I replied and said that I didn't think the club owed me anything but the respect I'd shown it over the years," he says. "We didn't have an argument. I was never brought up like that. So that was the frustrating thing that I was just discarded then."

After leaving City, Edghill had spells with Wigan, Sheffield United, QPR, Bradford and Macclesfield, before he retired in 2008. He's now back at Eastlands, entertaining fans in corporate hospitality on matchdays and showing visitors around as part of the 'legends tours' of the stadium and Carrington training ground.

"Since 2010, I've worked to get some of my coaching badges," he says. "I also work in a primary school in Harpurhey, doing the PE side of things of the curriculum and I do learning mentoring with some of the badly behaved children.

"I enjoy it," he says, "but by the time I get to Wednesday or

Thursday, I'm absolutely tired out! I end up saying the same things to the same children day in day out, breaking up fights, chasing kids who are running away from teachers, having to speak to kids every day about their behaviour... It's draining, but it's rewarding.

"As I always said when I started," he concludes, "if I can help one of them then I'll be happy."

4 GERARD WIEKENS

The plane touched down in Bremen, Germany and I let go of my dad's hand, having come close to ripping his knuckles out of their sockets throughout the whole of the flight's descent. I'm not a fan of flying. In fact, I hate it. I hate it so much that – on arranging an interview with Gerard Wiekens, now living and working back in his home country of the Netherlands – I made sure the dates tallied with when my father could book time off work just so I didn't have to fly alone.

From landing in Bremen, we took a three-hour coach journey across the Dutch border to Groningen, where our hotel was. Gerard lives nearby and I was due to meet him the following day. We checked in, enjoyed the evening meal and got our heads down for the night.

After breakfast the next morning, my mobile rang and Gerard told me he would come to the hotel. Roughly half an hour later, we met in reception and took a seat in the restaurant to have a chat about his time in England.

"It was difficult because I wasn't into English football that much," he says, "the only league you could see in Holland was the Premier League and City were playing in the First Division, so I didn't know what to expect. I looked on the internet, in the newspapers and magazines about City and found out that it was a big club – but I didn't know what to expect.

"I played in Holland for Veendam for seven years and was their best player. Every year there was interest in me from other clubs in Holland, but I was too expensive for them. Then suddenly [there was interest from] a club from abroad and it was difficult because I expected to play for another couple of years in Holland. I thought it was a really good chance and I wanted to go."

Wiekens made a big impression in his first match. Joining in the summer of 1997, he made his debut in the opening game of the

CITY CAREER STATS

Apps: 213 (18 sub)
Goals: 10

Signed: June 1997
Left: July 2004

Debut: Portsmouth (h), 1997
Result: 2-2 draw

following season and scored in a 2-2 draw with Portsmouth.

"When I arrived, they'd said they wanted to go straight back to the Premiership. If you look at the players they had and they bought, everything was ready for them to go back. But it was the other way around and we were relegated. Nobody expected it and it was very strange."

City underachieved during Wiekens' first season. Frank Clark had begun as the manager, but had lost his job in the February, when Joe Royle took over the reins. At the time of the managerial switch, City were second-bottom of the league and one point away from safety. The club had won just seven games of a possible 32 and the situation was looking bleak.

Come the final day of the season, the Blues travelled to Stoke. The Potters were a point ahead of City going into the game, but whoever won would escape relegation providing one of Portsmouth or Port Vale failed to win. Portsmouth travelled to mid-table Bradford, while Port Vale visited 15th-placed Huddersfield.

"You couldn't expect both to win," Wiekens recalls, "but they both won. We had a really good game against Stoke, but the atmosphere was strange. We won 5-2, but the fans were sad. It was a strange game. We won and a big club like City you'd never expect to go down to the Second Division, but it happened.

"The club is and was too big for the Second Division. Everybody expected us to come straight back up. But the first game, where we played Blackpool at home, was really difficult. I think even the players thought it would be easy to be champions."

City endured quite a poor start to the season. Following that opening day victory, the club won just four of their next 14 matches – a spell that included a five game winless streak and defeats at Maine Road against Preston and Reading.

Fortunes changed after Christmas, but Gerard couldn't explain why: "The only thing I can say is that we had a squad of players that were too good to play in the Second Division."

The turn of form saw City finish third – five points behind Walsall in second place and a huge 19 points off Kevin Keegan's runaway champions Fulham. That meant the lottery of the play-offs and a two-legged tie with sixth-placed Wigan. The first leg – which was the last game ever played at the old Springfield Park stadium – couldn't have got off to a worse start, as a mix-up between Wiekens and goalkeeper Nicky Weaver allowed the hosts to score within 19 seconds.

When I ask the Dutchman about it, I tell him I'd already got the goalkeeper's version of events. "So, he probably told you it was his fault?" Wiekens says with a cheeky grin on his face.

"We had a throw in and it came to me, but the ball was very fast. The striker [Stuart Barlow] was coming, so I pretended to kick it up field to clear it. I thought the ball was quick enough to go to the keeper so we could keep possession. But he also thought I was kicking it long, so he went backwards and Barlow got the ball and scored. It was a bad start.

"Paul Dickov scored the equaliser and I was very happy with that. After that game, a few days later, we had the player of the year do and they'd picked me. I heard fans talking about that game and that mistake, but it was too late to get another as player of the season!"

"...after the second goal, you think it's over and out. You could see the feelings of the fans – they left the stadium, they were moaning, they were unhappy. It's just a very bad feeling. You see another season in the Second Division and you didn't want that."

Dickov's equaliser, followed by Shaun Goater's dubious winner in the second leg, put the Blues into the final, where they would meet Gillingham – winners over Preston in the other semi-final.

"I can't remember much about the day itself," Wiekens says. "Like normal, I got nervous on the day of the game – but that's something you need as a professional player, I think. It makes you sharp and ready for it. But I can remember it was more than usual. It was a big game and my first time playing at Wembley. There were a lot of fans – on the way we saw them all going into the stadium. It was wonderful, but very, very nerve-racking.

"It was a terrible game from both sides," he recalls, "Gillingham didn't play well and we didn't play well. And then they scored and you think it's going to be very difficult to get promoted, but you try everything because one goal isn't that much."

He remembers the opening goal well: "I went to close down my opponent and he put it through my legs. It made me look bad," he says. "Even their second goal wasn't good defending. Not only me, but the whole team.

"But after the second goal, you think it's over and out. You could see the feelings of the fans – they left the stadium, they were moaning, they were unhappy. It's just a very bad feeling. You see another season in the

Second Division and you didn't want that."

How did he feel when Kevin Horlock pulled a goal back on 90 minutes? Did he think there was a chance the Blues would pull level?

"It was too late," he says, "we still had time, but you didn't expect it. It's a nice goal but it's 2-1 and you still lose.

"And then it was the last minute of injury time. I kicked a long ball to Gareth Taylor. He headed it on to the feet of Shaun Goater and he found Paul Dickov who scored. What you feel then is unbelievable: you've played 90 minutes, you're tired, and you didn't feel well because you're losing the game. Then he scores and you think you're going to do it. We were high and in the mood, and everybody thought that Gillingham were there, so it was a bad time for them."

There were few chances in extra time and the game went to penalties. "A few weeks before the final, we practised them in training every day and I was one of the penalty takers who scored a lot," Gerard tells me, "but I remember I had to take them with my old club in Holland and I missed half of them, so I wasn't feeling confident.

"They asked me if I wanted to take a penalty and I said, 'If I don't have to, I'd rather not.' It's nerve-wracking and I'm not good at that, so I didn't fancy myself.

"It was like a *Get Out Of Jail Free* card. At the start of the game, you think that if we win then we'll be in the First Division where the club belongs, maybe to go to the Premier League. Everybody thought it would be another year in the Second Division and I couldn't see myself playing there, I couldn't see City playing there. It was very disappointing and then suddenly we'd done it. That difference from being so down to being so happy made it even better."

Promotion brought new expectations the following season. The club had scraped out of the third tier at the first attempt and Gerard thought they would be consolidating their position in the higher league. In the end, the Blues finished second and earned back-to-back promotions, catapulting them into the top flight.

"We were lucky to get to the First Division and then you don't expect to be in the top two or three that season. But the players were good enough and the club was big enough to get there. I didn't expect it to be that quick."

The Dutchman missed out on the memorable final game of the season, when the Blues (somehow) won 4-1 at Ewood Park, despite being battered for the best part of an hour. In fact, Wiekens says that it was unbelievable City didn't go two or three down with the number of chances the hosts had had.

"The week before we trained in the stadium at Maine Road. We did some sprinting and I felt my hamstring. I knew straight away that I wasn't going to make the game. It was a really bad feeling."

For a man who – by his own admission – doesn't cope well with nerves, he says he hated being on the sidelines: "If you're not involved, you're more nervous because when you're on the pitch you can mean something for the team. You can do something. When you're not involved, you're helpless."

He remembers the day very clearly, though. He tells me about seeing City fans everywhere: "[Ewood Park] is a little bit in a slope. In the corners there were no stands, but there was a hill and it was full of City fans, all watching the game."

The City team that was promoted back to the Premier League that year was remarkably similar to the one that had contested the Division Two Play-Off Final in 1999. Back-to-back promotions launched them into the top league in the country, but the Blues weren't able to cope with the intensity of the opposition. A year to the day after going up at Blackburn, City were relegated at Ipswich – one match before the end of the season.

As a result, the board terminated Joe Royle's contract and took the club in a new direction.

"He [Royle] was a nice man," Wiekens says, "as a manager, I liked him. He was friendly, he was interested in your private life, and I had a really good time with him. Normally, when you play every game, you like the manager better than when you're a sub or if you're not playing, but it was great. He was a great man.

> "If you're not involved, you're more nervous because when you're on the pitch you can mean something for the team. You can do something. When you're not involved, you're helpless."

"When he was sacked, it was a shame. I don't know if he could have turned it around. In the end City did well, but it was sad to see him leave.

"I think when [Kevin] Keegan came, other players came," he continues, "better players, bigger players, players who had proved themselves already in the highest league. The wages went up. The whole club changed from a cosy, nice, friendly club to a more 'professional' one.

"Football, for me, is like a hobby. You do something you like and it's nice to do, and when Keegan came it was more like work. It wasn't as friendly and the team bonding wasn't the same as a few years before that. The atmosphere was different.

"My first year [under Keegan] was ok, but I didn't have a bond with him like I did with Joe Royle. I played a lot, but when you bring in big name players it's difficult to keep your place in the team. The second year, I played a lot less than the year before. It wasn't that nice for me at City at that moment."

> "The Manchester derby was my first game that season. It was strange because I didn't expect to play. I'm not sure if I was even on the bench for the games before and suddenly I had to start in the biggest game of that season."

Wiekens' chances in the first team became severely limited. Despite barely putting a foot wrong, he was seemingly left behind when Sylvain Distin joined the club and formed a strong partnership in defence with Steve Howey. With Richard Dunne also in the wings, the Dutchman had slipped down the pecking order.

Come the November of the 2002-03 season, though, and the Blues faced a defensive crisis. Both first choice centre backs limped out of a League Cup defeat at Wigan, four days before the first Manchester derby of the campaign. Instead of lining up against United with Howey and Distin across the back, the Blues threw in Lucien Mettomo (who had made just two other appearances that season) and Wiekens.

For such an important game, fans were worried the back four would be rusty – having barely played together and barely played at all in the build-up to the match. In the end, though, the Blues won 3-1.

"They [Distin and Howey] were both good defenders," Wiekens recalls, "if they're better than me, then they should be playing – that's normal. But, as a player, you want to play. You try hard, but it was difficult. I was around my 30s and wanted to play.

"The Manchester derby was my first game that season. It was strange because I didn't expect to play. I'm not sure if I was even on the bench for the games before and suddenly I had to start in the biggest game of that season. It was the last derby at Maine Road."

There was extra incentive for Wiekens to perform well in that game. Facing him was a striker who had been drawing all the plaudits since moving to Manchester United in 2001. He was also Dutch – and it was

Wiekens' job to mark Ruud van Nistelrooy.

"When he was playing in Holland for a small club called Den Bosch, I was playing for Veendam," Wiekens remembers, "we played against each other and I also had to mark him then. I did a good job then, too, and even scored the winning goal.

"So I was feeling ok. I'd played against him and I knew I could do well against him, but he's a great player and United were a great team. It was very difficult to get a result in that game, but it went well. I did well."

Perhaps understandably, Wiekens played down his performance in the Manchester derby. Having been thrown straight in at the deep end for that game, he didn't just keep his head above water, but managed to complete a hefty swim set too. Had it not been for Shaun Goater stealing the limelight with his 99th and 100th City goals, the Dutch defender could well have been named Man of the Match. There was certainly a strong case for it – van Nistelrooy didn't get a kick.

Despite such a good display, Wiekens made just six more appearances for the club in the remaining six months of that season. His final game for City was to come right at the start of the next campaign.

Having finished ninth, the Blues qualified for the UEFA Cup via the Fair Play League – judged not just on the number of cards a team has been shown, but also on how frequently they had put the ball out of play to help injured opponents, respect shown to officials or even the behaviour of the fans. The club had to enter the qualifying rounds, where they were drawn against Total Network Solutions from Wales (now renamed The New Saints).

In the first leg, Keegan fielded a full strength team. It meant that, by the time the second leg came around, the Blues were leaving Eastlands with a 5-0 aggregate lead. The reverse fixture was switched from TNS's home ground to the Millennium Stadium in Cardiff, to allow the Welsh side to open the gates for thousands more City fans than they could have done at the Recreation Ground.

Naturally, Keegan shuffled his pack – including Wiekens for the final time, where he was captain in a 2-0 City win.

"My contract was coming to an end that year," he says when I asked him if he realised, when walking off the pitch, that it might have been his last game for the club, "the year before I'd only played five or six games, so I knew it'd be very difficult to get into the team. You never know if it's your last game. I don't know how I was feeling. It was early in the season, but afterwards I never played again.

"I had a great time [at City]. I never expected to play abroad and I was 23 at that time, my wife – who was my girlfriend then – was 22. If you then have to go abroad just the two of you, it's not easy. But I have to say my seven years in Manchester were incredible. They were the best years of my life and the same for my wife.

"She was really finding it difficult for the first half a year," he continues. "When we went over, I met people and they took me to places, but she had to find her own way. But after that, she felt fine. Both or our kids were born in England and when we left she found it harder to leave than I did!

"On the pitch it was great, because I think football in England is the best in the world. The fans enjoy it – they live for it. Off the pitch, the people there are so friendly and they want to help you with everything. It was a great time."

When he was released at the end of his contract, Wiekens returned to the Netherlands and to the club where he started his career: FC Veendam. "It was a big change going back," he says. "It's a small club and if they had a good crowd it would be 3000 people, and for Veendam that's a massive crowd. Then to go to such a big club, the change was enormous and on the way back it was the same.

"I played professionally for 20 years and I had two clubs. For a professional footballer that played that long, it's strange. But when I feel at home somewhere, I like it and I want to stay."

"I knew what to expect. My first game I played for Veendam again was at Go Ahead Eagles and I was looking around and thought, 'What am I doing here?' because there was no atmosphere.

"I played professionally for 20 years and I had two clubs. For a professional footballer that played that long, it's strange. But when I feel at home somewhere, I like it and I want to stay. At Veendam they liked me and at City they liked me, so it was good."

When the interview had come to a close, Gerard made an offer that I just couldn't refuse. We'd wandered back to the reception area when I expected to shake his hand and we'd go our separate ways, but instead he invited both me and my dad on a tour of some of the parts of the region that are significant in his career. Ten minutes later, we were in his car and heading to the training pitches at FC Groningen – where he now works with the junior players.

It was on one of their plastic pitches where he explained why he finished his career refusing to play on artificial pitches: "It was summer. The pitch was dry and it was new. I had the ball at my feet and I wanted to kick it long. But at the last second spotted a run to my left. So I tried to switch it and turn to pass it there. I turned, but my foot stayed planted in the ground and I broke my leg, my fibula. That was the worst injury I had.

"I was 33 or 34 and I thought, 'I'm not playing on plastic grass anymore'. I think there were only one or two teams in Holland that played on that surface. I think I was the first player to refuse to play on it. It's not the same – when you make a sliding [tackle] or the smell... it's not nice.

"People thought I couldn't do it. Your team have to play the match and a lot of people got on my back [for the decision]. You never know for sure, but I think it [the injury] was caused by the artificial turf."

From there, we headed to the Green-White Army's stadium. To gauge the level of Groningen's team, my dad asks who Wiekens would compare them to in England. He tells us they're at a similar level to Everton – a team that performs well each season, but more often than not just misses out on European places. He tells us he was offered the chance to play there several times – but he turned them down each time out of loyalty to the team that had given him his first chance.

So, why is he now training the youth players at Groningen? The answer is quite a sad one – Veendam, where he spent roughly half of his life, no longer exists. In March 2013, the club went out of business, unable to pay debts of €675,000 and Wiekens was out of a job. It was then, with a heavy heart, he took up Groningen's offer.

He took us to the (now deserted) De Langeleegte stadium and explained all.

"After I finished playing, I came straight back as assistant manager [at Veendam], so I was helping the coach with the players I'd played with. For me it was good because when you play football for a long time and then stop, you feel an emptiness. But I didn't have it because I was still in the middle of the group.

"Every day, I was on the pitch and if there was a man short I was also training, so it kept me fit. It was very good and I did that for two and a half years at Veendam."

As we get out of the car at the stadium, there's an eeriness about the whole area. It's behind a residential street where life continues as normal. It's enclosed by trees, which hide it from the surrounding area, and there's an unusual quiet despite the busy road that runs beside it. We walk around the side and get a view of the pitch, but are unable to get any closer – the gates are bolted shut. I poke my camera through and take a photo of the bright yellow and black seats and the small part of the pitch that's in view.

"They were always struggling to get the finances right," Wiekens says. "At the end, with all the troubles with the companies, it was just a bad period for everyone. They didn't have the right money anymore and were declared bankrupt.

"It meant I lost a club, a place where I went for 22 years – and I'm 40, so it's a long period of my life. I went every day to that club and suddenly it's gone. Normally, when you stop and don't go to the club anymore, you miss it – but you can see games or go to training or whatever. But it's just gone. It leaves you with an emptiness inside."

And that led him to FC Groningen: "When I was a youth player with Veendam, FC Groningen – that was the biggest club in this area – wanted me as a youth player, but I chose to stay at Veendam. When I played in the first team, they were always interested and also when I stopped playing they wanted me to coach their youth.

"But because Veendam was in my heart, I stayed there. And then when they went bankrupt, they came back again and now I'm a coach for the Under-14s.

"When I was 15, I got into professional football and I'm still here. I can't see me doing anything else than being on the pitch, working with players and trying to make them better. It's great – I can't see me doing anything else, in an office or whatever. Thankfully, I'm still involved in football.

"I wasn't the best footballer. I don't have the technique to go around two people, to cross, to score... but the thing I had was attitude and mentality. That's more important. You can do tricks or something like that, but if you don't have the right mentality, you've got nothing.

"If you have a good mentality and

Deserted: De Langeleegte stadium sits unused in Veendam.

can play a little bit, you can get further."

It was a very strange atmosphere at the stadium and discussion turns towards similar examples of clubs struggling financially in England. Chester City – now Chester FC – went bust and reformed, while there was the season Portsmouth were close to going out of business whilst still in the Premier League. Wiekens even remembers when Stockport were in a higher league than City – but is shocked to hear they're now a part-time, non-league club in the Conference North, five divisions below the Blues.

As we get back into the car, I assume we're heading back to the hotel. The day's wearing on and the two bumbling idiots from England have taken enough of the former footballer's time, but he's got one more surprise in store for us. All the way, it felt like we were heading the wrong way for where we were staying and that hunch was correct, as we pulled into a residential area off the motorway and onto his driveway.

At his home, he's converted his garage into a memorabilia room – somewhere he keeps all his bits and bobs from his playing days. There are a few City shirts framed on the wall, and some from other Dutch players he's played with or against too. I spot Ruud van Nistelrooy's Manchester United shirt from the final derby at Maine Road, framed next to a Dirk Kuyt shirt from the national team.

There are photos from some of his best moments at City – including a goal at Stoke where he controlled and volleyed it into the net in 1998-99, plus a cracking challenge from the last Manchester derby at Maine Road. And there are his medals – Division Two Play-Off winner from 1999, Division One runner up from 2000 and Division One winner from 2002 – all of them framed and hung on the wall, too.

"I lost a club, a place where I went for 22 years – and I'm 40, so it's a long period of my life. I went every day to that club and suddenly it's gone."

He introduces us to his wife Angelique and we chat about how Manchester's changed since they left. They reminisce about times when George Weah was their next-door neighbour and about how they were able to settle in Cheadle, near to a place my dad used to play football.

Before we leave, I have to find out if they ever go back to England and if they ever visit to watch the club now. "Sometimes," he says, "it's always like coming home – I get to one or two games a season, but it's hard working in football.

"My sons are both City mad, though."

5 ANDY MORRISON

One of the biggest turning points in City's 1998-99 season, as has been described by several players and the manager himself, was the arrival of Andy Morrison from Huddersfield Town. He joined the Blues in October 1998 after a falling out with the Terriers' boss.

"I felt I'd been shown a lack of respect. I thought I'd been belittled in front of the players the night before," the central defender recalls. "I'm sure Peter Jackson, as he went on in his managerial career, would never have done what he did again – he would have dealt with it in a totally different way.

"The following day, we were back in and I went and spoke with him," he continues, "I didn't agree with what he said, I thought I was harshly treated and I ended up picking a table up.

"I got a phone call that afternoon and I was off to Man City on loan," he says.

He arrived at Maine Road in time for the club's home fixture with Colchester United. Kevin Horlock had put the home side a goal up four minutes after the break from the penalty spot, before – just four minutes later – the new signing bagged a goal on his debut.

"Sometimes in life things just happen the way they're meant to happen," he says, "I had a good debut and a great game. I scored, the fans took to me straight away, and that was fantastic. Sometimes things are just meant to be and at that period, it was meant to be. The chemistry was just right for both me and the club."

Morrison didn't have long to wait for his second goal, too. Visiting Boundary Park the following week, Kevin Horlock had again put City in front, before doubling the lead himself. As Oldham looked for a way back into the game, there was a goal of the season contender from the Blues' new signing.

"Back then," he says with a smile on his face, "it was roughly 22

CITY CAREER STATS

Apps: 48 (1 sub)
Goals: 5

Signed: October 1998
Left: July 2002

Debut: Colchester (h), 1998
Result: 2-1 victory

yards. Now the volley's nearly at 40 yards and I'm sure it'll soon have been from the halfway line! It was great because we were at Oldham, but the whole place was full of City fans, it was surreal. I was looking around, not sure where to run because they were everywhere.

"The ball came out from a set play and I just headed it back to Shaun [Goater]. Shaun headed it to me without it touching the ground and I volleyed it. Probably nine times out of ten, it'd have been heading down into the middle of Oldham, but this one I caught right and it just flew into the top corner."

But it wasn't all plain sailing for Morrison at City, even if it seemed like the club and the Scot had been a good match for each other.

Throughout his career he had faced problems off the pitch. From being thrown into the deep end of first team football at Plymouth, he was suddenly the subject of a transfer bid from Blackburn, who were building a squad to rival Manchester United in pursuit of the Premier League title. Soon after moving, however, the centre-back suffered an injury that would limit him to five appearances in the 1993-94 season. It was also around that time that he began to suffer with depression.

"I didn't deal with things well," he says, "when I was injured, it was a terrible and dark place. I was away from home and away from my family, and trying to adapt to life away with my son and my wife. As a footballer, you feel as if you're judged – which is wrong – and if you're not playing then you're no good to anyone. That's how I felt about myself back then.

"I slipped into depression and drink is never far away after that."

In his very frank and honest autobiography, the centre-back explains all about how he struggled with his battle with alcoholism throughout his career. While he was on the sidelines at Blackburn, there was one fateful trip back to Plymouth and an incident there in one bar that had seen Morrison arrested and charged with malicious wounding with intent. It was later described to him how serious the offence was.

"...if you're not playing then you're no good to anyone. That's how I felt about myself. I slipped into depression and drink is never far away after that."

"The reality of having a charge sheet read out and then your team say to you, 'You do realise that this is one below attempted murder?' and only after the court case did you look back and think. If you're found guilty of that, the game's up. Everything's over. It carries a maximum penalty of eight years in prison and my career would have been over."

This wasn't the first incident Morrison had been involved in, but it was the most serious. He was never found guilty of any, but he speculates that had he been, it might have been the wake-up call he needed to change his ways.

In his first appearance in the FA Cup for City, the defender was sent off by referee Graham Poll – who, Morrison says, told him afterwards that, when he reviewed what happened, he'd not even have booked him – for a something and nothing incident involving Wimbledon's Carl Cort. For a man who was getting everything in order on the pitch, off it the suspension was the last thing he needed.

"It gave me an opportunity to seek out what I did on many occasions when life caught up on me," he says. "I became restless, and irritable, and agitated, and I needed to get some sort of oblivion. I just needed to escape from life.

"I headed to Scotland. I'd already sorted out with Joe [Royle] to get the Monday off and off I went."

"I became restless, and irritable, and agitated, and I needed to get some sort of oblivion. I just needed to escape from life."

In his book, Morrison explains how he stopped for a drink in Inverness and woke up the next morning in a prison cell. There were six offences against his name, but was lucky to have had the charges dropped after a fight with a doorman, when the bar manager had seen that the footballer hadn't thrown the first punch. He paid for the damages, but continued to Kinlochbervie in the North West of Scotland, where his drinking continued. On one occasion, he spent the whole day in one bar until closing time, where he then bought 12 cans of lager and a half-full a bottle of vodka.

He stayed in his car and drank the lot, right through to sunrise the next day.

"That was the final piece to me to have to look at myself and look at the way I was living and my addiction problems. From there until this day, I've not touched, needed or wanted a drink of alcohol."

One key figure of Morrison's recovery was a fellow Scot, who was the Blues' then assistant manager. Joe Royle had brought Willie Donachie in as his number two soon after being appointed manager in February 1998.

"I can't over exaggerate how big a part Willie played in my life and my recovery," Morrison remembers, "he's a good man and he cares about his footballers as people as well. He likes to see people develop and to take a more philosophical approach to life. I really can't thank him enough."

Morrison was soon given the captaincy at City as he began to sort his off the field problems out. "I was very honoured to be given it by Joe," he says, "but I was also acutely aware of the responsibilities that came with it. The expectations of Manchester City were not to be playing in the league they were in."

This leads the discussion on to City's promotion push and him leading the team out at Wembley in May 1999. "When the realisation comes that you're in the play-offs, there is that feeling initially that it's a lottery and the stakes are high for each game. We knew a couple of weeks before that we'd be in the play-offs, so by the time they came around, we'd already prepared for it mentally. It wasn't like missing out on a result on the last Saturday of the season and dropping into the play-offs.

"I kind of limped through to the end of the season – I was waiting for my usual clean out in the summer," he says, talking about his knee, "I'd get through a season, have a clean out and be ready to go again and I was needing that. My knee was swollen. I had it drained and had a pain killing injection before the game and, to be honest, it numbed it completely.

"It wore off towards half time and I had some more put in," he continues, "I felt ok, but Joe said to me he felt like I looked like I was carrying it a bit in the second half. So he took me off and changed it around a bit."

Morrison left the action just after the hour mark, 20 minutes before Gillingham opened the scoring. For a man for whom 'actions rather than words' would be a fitting philosophy throughout his life, what was it like for him to have to watch the drama unfold and being unable to do anything about it from the bench?

"On a personal level, it felt like it wasn't part of the script," he says, "it wasn't how it was supposed to go – I'd turned my life around, we were going forward and it should have ended up with us getting promoted. Going 2-0 down wasn't part of the script.

"But we now know it was part of an ever better script! They just got a couple of quick goals that seemed to be at the right time for them. Nobody would think you're going to get back into it when they scored that late, you think the time's up.

"The lads dug in and found it from somewhere. It was the spirit of the club at the time, the spirit of the fans, and the coming together of everyone – the manager, the board, the fans, and the players. Everyone was in the boat together rowing in the same direction.

"To turn it around the way we did was beyond belief, really. Their bench were gone. When Paul [Dickov]'s goal went in, you could see it in the teamtalk. They were flat and they were shell-shocked. Even going into the penalties, I had no doubt [that City would win]."

I'm speaking to Morrison for the second time about his involvement in the Wembley game. The first was in 2011 for Imagine FM's *Blue Moon Live* show, while the second comes just days after the centre-back had appeared in a Former City XI vs. Former City XI friendly, as a testimonial for club kit man Les Chapman. In that game, held at Stockport County's Edgeley Park, Morrison belted a penalty into the top corner – so I ask him, had he still been on the Wembley pitch come the shootout, if he would have stepped forward for a spot-kick.

"If nobody else had stepped up, then I would take one," he says after a moment's thought, "but I would not be putting my hand up saying, 'I'll take one!' – not because I'm not brave enough to take one, but because I believe there are people better equipped to take a penalty than me. If I had to, I would – but it'd be in the latter stages and I wouldn't be one of the first five."

When the final penalty kick – from Gillingham's Guy Butters – was saved by Nicky Weaver, the young goalkeeper set off on a crazy run around the Wembley pitch. A mere 30 second later, he ran straight into Morrison, who gave him a good rugby tackle.

"The lads were chasing him around in a circle, but I was a bit older and a bit wiser, so I just cut him off. It was a massive pile-on," he says, laughing, "Nicky was at the bottom of it, fighting for his life, really! There must have been 20 people – I think the physio and the doc were on top, as well. I think he really struggled and then eventually got up and I asked if he was alright. He said he would be when I'd got off him!"

As his thoughts focus on the end of the game, Morrison begins to talk about the occasion. "You have your personal highs in your life," he says, "your marriage, your children, seeing your kids grow up – all of that. But on a football level, there's nothing to match them days. You'll never re-enact that. Anyone who has experienced a cup win or the winning of a championship... there's nothing to challenge that.

"It's a feeling of exhaustion almost when you're on the coach on the way back," he continues, "some of the lads (rightly so) would go out and have a party. I'd reached a point where I wasn't drinking and I was very much happy with myself that I'd achieved something at last. I'd made sacrifices and I felt like I'd been rewarded for that.

"Would I swap that for going straight up? Never would I take the automatic promotion! It was a really special day.

"In hindsight, you look back and think. I felt I'd made sacrifices and I'd not done that for anybody but myself. I was being right, being fit, and training and preparing right and being a leader. I was given that accolade [the captaincy] at many clubs, but I didn't always present myself in the right way off the pitch.

"Always on it, I never let anyone down. I never let teammates or myself down. But, away from football, many times I did and I didn't portray the image that a captain and professional footballer should do.

"So that game was like the payback for the sacrifices I'd made. I feel extremely proud that I've achieved something. I left Plymouth as a youngster to join Blackburn – a championship winning team – for my career to go forward, but my career stalled time and time again, not because of my ability but because of other antics. And I just had that feeling that I was at a huge club and I was the captain and that we were going to go into the next season and kick on."

City did exactly that. When many onlookers were expecting the Blues to consolidate their position in the First Division, the club

"I didn't lick him. It was nothing like the papers made out, sticking my tongue down his throat or anything like that. I think if the referee had remembered he'd already booked me, he probably wouldn't have sent me off. It was just one of those things that seem to follow me."

had different ideas. Despite having been seconds away from another season in the third tier, the team finished in second position to earn automatic promotion back to the Premier League. Over the course of two campaigns, the club had jumped from its lowest ever position back into the top flight.

Early in the season, City travelled to Fulham – who had been champions of the Second Division the year before – and there was controversy in store for Morrison once again.

The Cottagers had loaned a Premier League footballer that had been struggling for form with his parent club Aston Villa. Morrison had been giving Stan Collymore a tough time, winning the ball every time it came near and a war of attrition developed between them. In the second half, there was an incident that's often remembered as the City skipper licking the former Liverpool star's nose – though Morrison says otherwise.

"I didn't lick him. That's what people said, but I was just having general banter with Stan through the game and we had a slight fall-out. He made a few comments to me and my comment to him was, 'I've got you licked'. He'd not had a shot. He'd not had a kick.

"And he then said, 'What?' so I said it again and made a gesture of a lick. Then the referee pulled his book out and showed me a yellow card. Then he's put the card back in his hand and obviously seen that my name was on it already, so he's had to pull out a red card.

"It was nothing like the papers made out, sticking my tongue down his throat or anything like that," he continues, starting to smile. "I think if the referee had remembered he'd already booked me, he probably wouldn't have sent me off. It was just one of those things that seem to follow me."

As that season progressed, City continued to perform well. But how much had changed at the club from the year before?

"We brought Mark Kennedy in, who was a colourful character around the place," he says, "he was what we needed and he brought real quality. I think Mark probably, at the time, would have been one of the first people to admit that his career was underachieving and was stalling, but everyone could see his potential. He came to City and whether it was Joe, Willie, the fans... whatever... it seemed to ignite his career again.

"Richard Jobson also came back from an injury that he'd had the season before," the ex-skipper continues, "and he was as good as any centre half in the country. He had injuries and his age was catching up with him, but he was another that had a fantastic season.

"We had momentum and enthusiasm," he says, "there was a fantastic team spirit. It was 'Manchester City: a club going forward' rather than 'Manchester City: a club in decline'. People wanted to come and play for us, where the season before they'd been linked and ended up moving to Barnsley and places like that."

As the squad progressed up the leagues and were back in the Premier League, there were criticisms from outside about what became dubbed as a 'drinking culture'. Morrison – as a recovering alcoholic – was surrounded by the late 90s party atmosphere, so was it difficult for him?

"I didn't [struggle]. I look back now and I do think I took the holier than thou attitude and I was like the reformed smoker who hates people smoking around them. I didn't agree with it, but we were being successful and we were winning games. There was a fantastic team spirit – and the lads were no different to any other team. They liked to have a drink. They worked hard and they played hard.

"It's well known that if you're winning games of football, you can get away with murder. You could run up and down Deansgate with no clothes on and it'd just be exuberance and high spirits – that's what lads do.

"But if you're struggling and down the bottom, then it's totally unacceptable in the public's eye.

"That was the difference [between the 1999-2000 promotion season and the 2000-01 relegation season], because the drinking was no different. The way the boys celebrated a win or had a night out on a Tuesday or a Sunday afternoon was no different to the season before.

"If anything, it had calmed down from the season before, but because we were struggling and because of the size of the club, the press will get something and go after it. They made a big issue out of something that had been no different to the previous season when we were winning games."

While City were struggling in the top flight, Morrison was struggling to get much game time for the Blues. Following an injury he had sustained towards the end of the 1999-2000 campaign, he was finding it difficult to get back fully fit and then to get back into the team.

"The club had brought players in," he says, "as a centre half, it would always have been difficult for me, at that age and that time of my career, to go on and establish myself. In my younger days, playing in midfield, I believe I could have held my own at any level. To play centre half in the Premier League you need to have pace. You need to be comfy in one-on-one situations. And I never had the pace to do that.

"I accepted that at the time. Joe tried to adapt the team to fit me in by playing a back three and the games I played I didn't let anyone down. But, looking at the long term, it would have been hard for me in the Premier League to hold my own.

"I played against Coventry and against Birmingham in the cup and scored – and I had a fantastic game. I felt like things were going in the right direction. I went out on loan and got myself fit," he says. "Of course the injuries would hold you back, because you lose the momentum. If you've been out for as long as I was at times – two, three, four months – you need six months to be match fit, to be sharp, for everything to be right.

"I got back fit and my knee went again. And I was never going to get back fully fit after the final time, there was just too much damage done. I believe had I been fit and been in the team from Christmas, we'd have stayed up.

"We had good players there, but I thought they'd begun to lack a little bit of the spirit. That team had been broken up, which it always was going to be broken up. Other players came in – the likes of George Weah or Paulo Wanchope – and, for me, the team lost a little bit of spirit."

Morrison's final game for the club was to come at Anfield in an FA Cup tie. The Blues went on to lose 4-2 and the captain, who had started the game, was substituted off on the hour mark. He has mixed memories about that day.

"Although it's not right," he says, "but the players who will come off, if the manager has to make a 50-50 decision on taking one or two players off, and one player will look at him and throw his arms in the air, walk off the pitch shaking his head, reluctantly shake the manager's hand and then sit down with a sulk, or another player will jog off the pitch, applaud the fans and sit down – the latter will be the one who goes off. The manager doesn't need to have that hassle.

"I felt it was an easy option to take me off and I said that to Joe," he continues, "I said I was unhappy about it and I got a load of abuse off the Liverpool fans when I sat down. So I picked my bottle of water up and sprayed it all over them, just to antagonise them and be me."

While Morrison had his disagreements with the manager, his relationship with Royle was different to that he'd had with any of his other bosses. The defender says it was similar to the relationship he had with Willie Donachie.

> "I got a load of abuse off the Liverpool fans when I sat down. So I picked my bottle of water up and sprayed it all over them, just to antagonise them and be me."

"I genuinely felt like Joe cared," he says. "When I had my last episode of drinking, he never came with the big book and a fine, reading the riot act to me. He approached it more from a 'forget about the football, do you not think you deserve a better quality of life than this?' standpoint. And it was the first time I'd looked at it in that way.

"It wasn't, 'I need to sort myself out because I play for this club' or, 'I need to sort myself out because this is unacceptable', but it was about me. I'd always tried to stop drinking and stop my unacceptable behaviour for other people, but this time I decided it had to be for me. And that's why it [the relationship with the manager] was different."

Looking back over his time with City, Morrison has good memories. He was a huge part in the team that turned the club's fortunes around and got them back on the map when they were close to breaking point.

"It made the club appealing to investors," he says, "Kevin Keegan came in and he was given a far, far bigger budget than what Joe Royle was working with. He got the club up and they walked the First Division the following season, with a record points total and record goals.

> "I genuinely felt like Joe [Royle] cared. When I had my last episode of drinking, he never came with the big book and a fine, reading the riot act to me. He approached it more from a 'forget about the football, do you not think you deserve a better quality of life than this?' standpoint."

"They had established themselves in the Premier League and were a top ten side. Unless you fall on a good crop of youngsters or you get a major investor – something needs to happen – that's where the club would have been. Then, obviously, when the investment's come from Abu Dhabi, it kicked the club to the next level.

"But that would never have happened but for that group of players and those fans as well. Those fans that stuck with the club – we had 30-odd thousand from January onwards. Every game was a sell-out. I'll never forget that incredible loyalty. Hell or high water, shit or champagne, they were always there.

"If any group of fans deserved to be buying the players the club are buying now or sticking their chests out saying, 'That's my football club, look where we are now', then it's them fans. They're entitled to that, because they were having to say that when we were halfway down the Second Division and those across the road were winning the treble."

Having finished his playing career, Morrison was assistant manager to Andy Preece at, first Worcester City, and then Northwich Victoria. However, at the time of our interview, he's moved to the Welsh league and is at Airbus.

"No opportunities were really opening themselves up," he says, talking about the English league, "it's not a closed shop, but it's very much about who you know and your contacts. So we moved across to the Welsh league to try and get a side that hadn't been in the top ten up challenging for a European place.

"In our first season, we came runners up. We've taken the club on leaps and bounds – it's a different type of club from what it was when we came in. The club have backed us now to bring in better players and we have to try and keep that momentum going.

"They say it's the next best thing to playing," he says, when I ask how he's coping with not being out on the pitch, "I enjoy it. It can be frustrating as well as fulfilling. You go from one Saturday banging your head against the wall to the next being elated. I enjoy the intensity that comes from the Welsh league."

If reports are to be believed, Morrison's spell with Preece wasn't his first stint at management. In 2010, he was appointed as the boss for the Seychelles national team – except he wasn't; it was a case of mistaken identity. In fact, their FA had approached a man called Andrew Amers Morrison, who ran a samba soccer school for underprivileged kids in London, thinking it was the former defender.

"I did [take the job] if he was successful and won a few games and maybe qualified for a competition," he says, laughing, "I'd have used that on my CV. Fair play to him, if he got a bit of sun and a few pina coladas off the back of it, then fair play."

As seems to be the way with the kids of the 1999 team, his son is another who is a City fan. So, at the end of the 2011-12 season, were the club ever going to win the Premier League in any other way than by needing two goals going into stoppage time?

"It makes you think exactly who's pulling the strings in the grand scheme of things," he says. "I've experienced it as a player and then I experienced it as a fan with my son. It was surreal, really, for Edin Dzeko to score the goal that just seemed to be a consolation – the same as what Kevin Horlock's goal was. And Dzeko will probably be remembered similar to Horlock.

"It was about Sergio Aguero and Paul Dickov," he continues, "it was staggering. And to see the reaction of grown men and women around me, it really was special. It was another feeling of relief.

"We turned up at the QPR game expecting to win and I'm as guilty as anyone – I did an interview before the game about this being our destiny and how we'd worked so long for this, how this was a different Manchester City with new players and one that doesn't fall flat on its face. And there we were again.

"For me, it wasn't about celebration. It was relief."

6 KEVIN HORLOCK

"I know this sounds terrible, but I still didn't think that was enough. I didn't envisage what was going to happen after that. I thought the time was up. On a personal point – and I know it sounds dreadfully selfish – I thought, 'We've had a terrible day, but I've scored at Wembley and I can tell the grandkids that.'"

We're sitting in a downstairs room of Needham Market FC's clubhouse and, naturally, there's only one place where the discussion could start. Just like Kevin Horlock on the pitch, when his goal at Wembley in 1999 hit the back of the net, there were few in the stands that celebrated it. With the board for stoppage time being raised and the goal pulling the score back to 2-1, thousands of fans thought it was too little, too late.

CITY CAREER STATS

Apps: 232 (21 sub)
Goals: 41

Signed: January 1997
Left: August 2003

Debut: Oxford Utd (a), 1998
Result: 4-1 victory

"Obviously it's an even better story to tell the grandkids, now!" He adds, after a moment's pause.

"All I remember was that, as a player, you really want to try and get back into the match. I remember trying to cover as much ground as I could. When we were defending, I tried to get back – because, obviously we couldn't concede another one.

"Then I just remember the ball breaking forward and thinking I needed to get to the edge of the area as quickly as I could. Obviously, I'm not the quickest player in the world. Luckily enough, maybe being a bit slower helped me run onto the ball, rather than have to backpedal for it.

"I remember arriving and the ball just seemed to come across for me. All I was thinking was just, 'Hit the target – head down, get a good connection and hit the target'.

"It was a good strike. You can look at it as quite a good goal, I suppose, because I stayed quite composed – but maybe that was due to the fact I thought the game was over anyway! Maybe if it was to equalise like Dicky's was, I'd have probably skied it!"

Even through chatting to him for a brief few moments, I can tell that Horlock is the joker in the pack. There's a cheeky charm about the way he talks and he's very humble about his own contributions to the City team that won promotion in 1999. When we first met – in the bar area of Needham Market's clubhouse – he was clearly well liked by the staff and players that were there. As he walked in, three players, who'd been on the pool table, immediately started a game of 'one-upmanship' with him, ribbing him about his pool-playing ability. And Horlock gave as good as he got back, too.

He's capable of serious, too, though. After talking about his goal, we started talking about the bigger picture with regards to that match.

"We realised what a big game it was," he says, "not only in that season but in the history of the club. If we'd have languished in that division for much longer, then who knows what would have happened? We knew we had to get out at all costs – and it did go down to the last game.

> "I just said to Jeff [Whitley], 'I'm not going in, I'm going to stay out here for as long as possible.' And Jeff being Jeff said he was staying out as well and it turned into a bit of a standoff as to who was going to stay in the rain the longest. And when I say rain, it was unbelievable. It was torrential."

"I sensed there was a little bit of tension, knowing that we were massive favourites. We had everything to lose and nothing to win, really. I sensed that amongst the lads and certainly felt that way myself.

"We tried to keep preparations as low key as possible," he says. "Joe [Royle] was good at that. He kept the pressure off the boys and maybe that's where I came into his plans a little bit.

"Joe didn't sign me at Ipswich [in 2004] just because of the player I was," he explains, "I think he saw me as a person who could take the pressure off. I used to have a laugh in the dressing room; I used to have a bit of fun. And speaking to people in Ipswich now, he actually signed me for that reason. Not just my footballing ability.

"So, Joe kept it low-key and I tried to keep it that way, too. It was a game we had to win and that adds pressure in itself, without having to deal with the opposition and Gillingham were a big, strong team."

What Horlock doesn't realise at this point is that I had already spoken to Joe Royle. I have to ask him about an incident that I'd been told about by the then City manager.

"We'd been out for a walk," the former midfielder says, "we'd got down to the hotel and we'd all gone out for a walk and had a cup of coffee down the road. On the way back, there was a monsoon. It was torrential rain. A few of the boys rushed in, but – and this will sound pretty immature now – me and Jeff [Whitley] were stood there.

"There were a few tourists taking pictures of the rain. Then eventually they were taking pictures of me and Jeff because we looked bloody idiots, to be fair!

"I just said to Jeff, 'I'm not going in, I'm going to stay out here for as long as possible.' And Jeff being Jeff said he was staying out as well and it turned into a bit of a standoff as to who was going to stay in the rain the longest. And when I say rain, it was unbelievable. It was torrential.

"We were stood there getting drenched and I looked over Jeff's shoulder and the manager was the other side of the glass window of the hotel saying, 'Get yourself in here now!' So then it became survival of the bravest."

A wry smile appears on his face as he adds, "Jeff went in first."

Horlock joined City from Swindon Town in January 1997, for a fee reported to be between £1.25m and £1.5m. At the time, the club were struggling in Division One when they had been expected to be fighting for promotion. He was the first player brought in by Frank Clark and later described by then chairman Francis Lee as one of only two good signings the manager had made for the club.

"Without sounding too big-headed, I had a few options open to me," Horlock says about making the move to Maine Road, "I was scoring a lot of goals at Swindon and there were a few clubs – like most clubs – interested in a goalscoring midfielder.

"Steve McMahon was my manager at Swindon and he rang me on the Thursday morning and said they'd had a bid from Manchester City and another club. He said, 'We've accepted Man City's offer, so you can go and speak to them.' I was a young boy, so I asked him what he would do.

"He said, 'If I were you, I'd go and speak to Manchester City.' There were a couple of Premier League teams interested in me, too. He said, 'It's a massive club, yes they're not in the top division, but that doesn't mean anything. Go and speak to them.'

"So I drove up in my sponsored Swindon car," he continues, "and signed that evening. I made my mind up straight away. I met Frank Clark and Franny Lee, they sold it to me and, looking back, I'm chuffed that I signed."

We talk a little bit about how the club struggled during the time of his arrival. At the end of his first half-season at Maine Road, the Blues finished in mid-table despite being preseason favourites to win the division. At the end of his first full campaign with the club, he suffered relegation.

He had become a regular first team player by the 1997-98 season, though an injury saw him missing four months of football. While he was out, Frank Clark was sacked and Joe Royle took the helm.

> "We knew we had to get out of that division. It's difficult because of the disappointment of the season before and getting relegated at Stoke was a massive blow."

"Obviously I hadn't been at the club when they'd experienced the highs of a few years earlier," he says, "there were a few big names and I hadn't seen that. I came from a smaller club in Swindon Town, so to me it was big and brand new and exciting. It was something I was really looking forward to.

"It was only a little bit further down the line that we did drop down that I realised what a fairly big mess we were getting into."

And it was a mess. The club had a long list of senior professional players – some internationals – who couldn't even get a reserve team match thanks to the size of the squad, while the final day of the season relegation to Division Two left them facing the worst times in their history. When Horlock added City's fifth against Stoke, the celebrations showed how much the players at the time understood the problems – they were muted, showing they were well aware that whatever they did that afternoon, results elsewhere had gone against them. The reality of a future in the English third tier was dawning on the squad.

"Every season, you set targets," Horlock says, talking about the start to the 1998-99 campaign, "it's always to be successful, obviously. We knew we had to get out of that division. It's difficult because of the disappointment of the season before and getting relegated at Stoke was a massive blow.

"Obviously, players left and you regroup and try and pull yourself together. We found it difficult. Although, on our day, we were the best team in that division by a mile – even though good players had left. But we were everybody's cup final. We were going to away games, smaller grounds, taking full crowds with us, and it added to the atmosphere and it piled the pressure on.

"Although we should have been able to deal with it, at times it did get to us. There was a lot of responsibility on our shoulders to get out of that division. At times, it didn't quite happen for us. Fortunately for us, it did in the end."

It took a monumental turn in form the Blues to be in with a chance of automatic promotion at the end of that season. It would turn out to have begun slightly too late, leaving the club destined to finish in third place and face the play-offs.

However, in the February of that season, and smack bang in the middle of that run of form, City travelled to Dean Court to face Bournemouth. In the end, the Blues would draw 0-0, but it would turn out to be a very welcome point after a truly bizarre refereeing decision – one Horlock would never forget.

When I ask about it, he laughs. "Where do I start?" he says.

"It was a big crowd and the majority were City fans," he explains, "I don't know whether it got to the ref. Jamie Pollock had just been sent off and there'd been a few dodgy tackles flying around – like I said, we were big fish in a small pond and everyone wanted to kick us and everyone wanted to beat us.

"There was a break-up in play," he continues, "I don't know what had happened, I think someone had gone down injured. But there'd been a tackle about a minute before on the halfway line and I was just walking towards the ref to question it. I didn't even speak and that's the craziest thing. In his report, it said I didn't say anything to him. I was

"...the referee's report came through and his words were that he'd sent me off for walking towards him in an aggressive manner. Which is bizarre, isn't it?"

walking towards him and he just flashed the [red] card at me."

He says he didn't think the card was for him at first: "I've not seen footage of it since, but I've looked over my shoulder thinking he's thrown it at someone who's behind me.

"He said, 'No, you, off you go!'

"And I said, 'What for?' and he replied, 'Off you go'.

"So I've wondered what was going on. I've walked off into the dressing room and Jamie Pollock was getting out of the shower having been sent off previously and he said to me, 'What've you been sent off for?' and my answer was, 'I actually don't know.'

"Joe [Royle] has come in after the game and said to me, 'What did you say?' and I said to him, 'I didn't actually say anything!' He said, 'You must have sworn at him,' and I replied, 'I didn't say anything to him.'

"Then the referee's report came through and his words were that he'd sent me off for walking towards him in an aggressive manner. Which is bizarre, isn't it? I walked fairly quickly towards him, maybe. I've got one leg shorter than the other, so maybe it looked like I was being a little bit aggressive.

"But I was just going to ask him about a foul previously. It's something that everyone remembers and it's funny now. But it wasn't at the time when I ended up missing a few games because of it."

Despite the Blues' good form, a defeat against Wycombe followed by a draw with Bristol Rovers meant that, on the final day of the season, no matter what their result was against York, City would be in the play-offs. Horlock remembers the run-in well.

"A friend of mine was playing for Walsall at the time and they were the team that ended up going up [in second place]," he says. "It was away to Wrexham [when the turnaround in form began], I think. It was Boxing Day. I took a corner and Gerard Wiekens scored and from that day we went on a mad run of winning games and it did look like we might sneak in.

"The worrying thing about that is that you get so close and have that disappointment, it can have a negative effect on you going into the play-offs. You're on a low, while someone who sneaked into the play-offs is on a high. We knew it was all to play for and we knew if we performed well we'd have a good chance of winning them."

The Blues went into the play-offs – as they had done most games that season – as favourites. Horlock says he knew the club had to be careful not to get complacent because they were always up against it and under pressure: "Everybody wanted to see us fail. Everyone wanted us to come out with egg on our faces. We were the big club in a small pond.

"In all honesty, I don't remember a lot about the game," he says of the Play-Off Final, "I remember my terrible miss with a header that I hit straight at the goalkeeper and – obviously – the ending.

"The actual walk out onto the pitch was special. Not just that, it was the whole turning up at Wembley and seeing all the fans there, especially after what we'd put them through that season – the grounds we'd been to, the teams we'd lost to that, without disrespecting them, we should never have even been playing. But we'd put ourselves in that position, so turning up and seeing the support we had was overwhelming.

"Then walking out onto the pitch was a special moment. The end was special, too. The middle bit wasn't, if I'm honest.

"When they scored their first one, I just always believed we'd get back in it. We had that fighting spirit and we'd shown it that year. So I still thought we'd get back in it, but once they scored the second, I thought that was it. Everybody did, even Gillingham.

"I'll never forget it. I remember the ball got cleared down to our left back position and it rolled out of play and we had a throw in down by our own corner flag. I turned and I thought, 'We're going to have to go back to all these clubs, what's happened?' And I remember looking up and seeing their two centre halves cuddling each other and jumping up and down on the spot.

"That will always stick with me because the disappointment I felt at that moment was incredible."

Seconds after Horlock had netted, the fourth official held the board up to show five minutes of stoppage time. With the score now at 2-1 and with City's tails up, the Blues were in the ascendancy. The midfielder remembers his reaction: "I think it galvanised the team and I think it knocked the stuffing out of Gillingham.

"They'd made a lot of substitutions. They'd taken their forwards off and didn't have any real offensive threat to us then. So it was a matter of them trying to hold on and, as everybody knows, if you're trying to hold on to something, it's very difficult if a team's camped in your half.

"We threw everything at them and had a few half chances before Dicky scored. If you wanted a chance to fall to anyone, it was Dicky. He was tenacious, he was always on your shoulder and ready for anything to drop. Luckily enough it did and it was a great finish.

"To be fair, I mention

"I thought, 'We're going to have to go back to all these clubs, what's happened?' And I remember looking up and seeing their two centre halves cuddling each other and jumping up and down on the spot. That will always stick with me because the disappointment I felt at that moment was incredible."

his goal more than mine! Obviously, nobody remembers mine. I actually had a touch in the build-up to his – and it's hard to see in the video. The ball's come up and I've just touched it around the corner to Goat, I think. Obviously, Goat's been tackled. Then I just remember him [Dickov] striking through the ball and seeing the net rippling.

"Dicky's run off and there's that famous picture of him sliding on his knees. I don't mention this too often, but me being a little bit slower and having a really bad ankle at the time from a kick on it in the game, by the time I got to the celebration, everyone was half getting up. Dicky went to throw his arm into the air as he celebrated and he slipped and lost his footing and fell on his face.

"Nobody really saw it and I laughed to him as we were going back to the halfway line. I don't think anybody else saw it. I don't think it was caught on camera. I don't think the fans saw it because they were ecstatic and jumping about in the stands. The lads that had been celebrating at the start had been going back to their positions. But I'd like to think Dicky remembers it, it was quite funny."

> "...by the time I got to the celebration, everyone was half getting up. Dicky went to throw his arm into the air as he celebrated and he slipped and lost his footing and fell on his face. I don't think anyone else saw it."

Extra time in the game became something of a non-event. Gillingham carried little threat having tried – and failed – to defend their lead. City, meanwhile, had been all-out attack and looked concerned about breakaways.

"In hindsight," Horlock says, "I wasn't disappointed not to have won it in extra time because then we wouldn't have had the excitement of penalties. But I think we'd worked so hard to get back into it, it got to the stage where both teams didn't want to lose. It became a bit of a stalemate and it was a bit boring. I think both teams had settled for penalties and would deal with it that way."

When the final whistle went on extra time, the manager had to pick his five takers for the spot-kicks. Horlock had been the regular penalty taker throughout the season, so he was aware he'd be facing some of the responsibility.

"Yeah, I knew I'd be involved," he says, "I think it's important that whoever takes them has got to want to take one. You can't really have someone going up if they're not really sure if they're confident enough. And, to be fair, I'd missed penalties. I think it says in the commentary, I'd missed the one before.

"So I wasn't a hotshot penalty taker," he continues, "but I was confident enough. I was brave enough. I was one of the older players in the group, so I said I'd go up first."

Horlock's penalty was dispatched neatly, but it was the second and fourth kicks of the afternoon that stick vividly in his mind. "I've never seen that before in my time," Horlock says of Dickov's kick that hit both posts and stayed out. "But, what about Richard Edghill's? Top corner! That was more surprising!"

Following the high of that penalty shootout victory, the Blues continued their run of good form into the next season in Division One. Despite being newly promoted, they ended the season in second place. In two seasons, they'd gone from the third tier of English football to the top flight. As Horlock explains, confidence was high.

"We just aimed to be successful," he says, "I think, as a team coming up, obviously you have to be a little bit sensible because we'd lost a few players from the year before and you're trying to galvanise and bring in better players. But I think that, with the backing we had and the support we had, we had to think play-offs.

"To the outside world, you'd say play-offs, but in the camp we would have wanted to be promoted as champions."

It seemed, though, that City don't do promotions the easy way. Beginning the final day of the 1999-2000 season in second place, they simply needed a draw to confirm that they would stay above Ipswich. The Blues were away at Blackburn, while the Tractor Boys were hosting Walsall at Portman Road.

The news at half time wasn't good. City had fallen behind to a first half Matt Jansen goal, while David Johnson had scored for Ipswich – as it stood, it would be the Blues in the play-offs once again.

"If I'm totally honest, it felt like it was going to go wrong," Horlock says, "but I'd had that feeling the year before, so it certainly didn't mean that I was going to give up."

When I'd asked the question about the game to the former midfielder, I'd used the phrase "Blackburn had battered City" in the first half. In response, Horlock says that I "underestimated it" with the amount of chances the home side had had.

"I can't remember how many times they hit the post. It just felt like it was hitting the woodwork all the time. Then when we went behind, we had to ask ourselves whether there was enough left in us to get back in it. A few of us probably shied away from it on the day and didn't perform as well as we could have, whether it was nerves or being scared of failure, I'm not sure.

"As soon as we got back in it and once we'd got our noses in front, everyone wanted the ball and to be a part of it. It was another special day."

To make it 1-1 at Ewood Park – in what would eventually be a 4-1 victory for the away side – Shaun Goater netted from a low ball through the box, played in by Kevin Horlock.

"I can't remember how many times they hit the post. It just felt like it was hitting the woodwork all the time. Then when we went behind, we had to ask ourselves whether there was enough left in us to get back in it."

"Similar to the Gillingham game, I was just trying to cover as much ground as possible," he says, "I think Mark Kennedy went down the left and he was a fairly quick player – although they all were compared to me! I just remember backing him up and he rolled it inside to me. And we all know what the Goat was about – if the ball goes in the box, he's going to be there or thereabouts. So I just put it into that area.

"I was always told as a young lad that if you're in a crossing position, put it in between the goalkeeper and the back four. The defenders don't want to defend it, the goalie can't come for it and looking back it was probably textbook 'corridor of uncertainty' where nobody could deal with it.

"Goat's just peeled off round the back and that was an easy finish for him. That was what he was all about and we knew that if we got him on the ball in good areas, he'd always get us back in it."

That promotion meant that the team that would be competing in the Premier League in 2000-01 was only a few players different to the one that had been ever so close to losing the 1999 Division Two Play-Off Final.

"It was crazy," Horlock says, "obviously, it's the place where everybody wants to play football. To get promoted and then do it again with not many changes was special, really – but maybe that says we shouldn't have got into the position we did the years before.

"But all's well that ends well and we got the club back to where it should be," he continues. "It's where the club deserved to be and where the fans deserved to be watching their team play.

"It's a massive part of my life and it was life-changing to say I was part of that.

"It was a special team spirit and I mention it to my boys here all the time," he says, nodding towards the stairs leading up to where some Needham Market players were still on the pool table. "We had some good players, but I think a lot of our togetherness and team-spirit got us through. You can have a good team, but if you've not got team-spirit, then you haven't got a lot.

"We definitely had it. We never knew when we were done. We weren't all mates and we weren't all sociable with each other outside of football, but when we trained and when we played we were one. And I think that showed."

Horlock was at City during one of the most – if not the most – turbulent times in their history. In fact, after arriving in 1997, the midfielder experienced two relegations and three promotions in his time with the club. His second relegation came at the end of the 2000-01 season, when – a year to the day after that promotion at Blackburn – the Blues lost at Portman Road. That 2-1 defeat at Ipswich meant they couldn't escape the Premier League's bottom three on the final day of the campaign.

"It was mad," he says, "when you're involved in it, you just get on with it and think it's normal. Looking back now, though, I'd never change it. At the time, getting relegated is a horrible, horrible feeling. But looking back at it when it's all done and dusted – and seeing where the club is now – I wouldn't change it."

At the end of that Premier League relegation season, the Blues made another change. Manager Joe Royle lost his job and Kevin Keegan came in to take the reins at Maine Road. For Horlock, it was his second managerial change at the club.

"It's disappointing whenever you see a manager lose his job," he says, "especially when you don't expect it and it comes out of the blue. Joe was a top man and I've got a lot of respect for him. He brought me to Ipswich as well, so I had quite a good relationship with him.

"But it sometimes does give the club a lift when a new manager comes in, especially as big a name as Kevin Keegan. It gave the whole place a boost and, in hindsight, maybe it was the right thing to do."

The following promotion season, where the Blues went on to win the Division One title playing some ridiculously good football, is one that sticks in the minds of many fans, perhaps only bettered by the 2011-12 Premier League title campaign in recent years.

"I know it's not the Premier League, but in Division One at that time, it was like the dream team," Horlock says, remembering playing with the likes of Eyal Berkovic or Ali Benarbia. "It was unbelievable to be a part of. He got us playing football like I'd never really been involved with before. Thankfully, Keegan made me a fairly big part of it – I played in the middle with some unbelievable players and I enjoyed every minute of it.

"It was fun. At times, we became a little bit arrogant in many ways because we knew we were going to go and win games," he continues, "it was a massive contrast to the Division Two season when we were nervous, we just used to go out onto the pitch and we knew we were going to batter teams.

> "It was fun. At times, we became a little bit arrogant in many ways because we knew we were going to go and win games. It was a massive contrast to the Division Two season when we were nervous..."

"I think we went into that [2002-03 Premier League] campaign a lot more confidently. We had a better squad that could probably cope with it more. We had some big names in there as well that were proven in the Premier League, which we didn't have before. So we were more armoured to deal with it and we proved that."

City finished ninth in their return to the top flight under Keegan. During the final season at Maine Road, there were some memorable games – with the stand-outs probably being the two Manchester derbies, where the Blues won 3-1 at home and drew 1-1 away.

But for Horlock, the games often blended into one: "I don't remember too much about them, if I'm honest. The biggest one I remember is the final game at Maine Road. I'd been at the club a long time and I was desperate to be a part of it. When I wasn't, it was fairly upsetting if I'm honest.

"A young Joey Barton had been coming through the ranks and doing well, which you accept as a player," he continues. "I was hoping that because I'd been there a long time and I was the longest serving player at the time, Keegan may have played me in it.

"And the final Manchester derby at Maine Road, I started as a sub for," he says, "I didn't get to play in too many derbies – I think I started one at Old Trafford. Joe [Royle] left me out of one at Maine Road, so in terms of derbies, I didn't have that much to do with them, if I'm honest.

"I remember coming on as sub in it [the final derby at Maine Road] and I remember [John] O'Shea had a chance to score late on in it," he says, "I was on that post and it went over, but that was my last memory of it."

The emergence of Joey Barton was where Horlock's City career began to end. With first team opportunities limited, he left to return to his first club, West Ham.

"In hindsight, I should never have done," he says, "I still had two years left at City and I've said it in interviews before, but I realised that I was a fairly good Championship player. As a Premiership player, I was probably a little bit short and I'm honest about that and big enough to say that.

"Keegan pulled me and said that I wasn't going to play as many games the next season. He said they were looking to blood Barton into the team, so I just thought the time was right for me to leave and with it being West Ham – which was the club I supported as a kid – made the decision a little bit easier.

"**"I got as fit as I'd been for years and years. And then on my second day back, I was messing around on the training ground, obviously being excited that my knee was good, and I dived into a puddle and dislocated my shoulder. And that more or less ended my career."**

"Looking back, it wasn't the right decision because the managers changed at West Ham and I quickly found myself out of favour.

"I moved on to Ipswich with Joe [Royle], which was good and I enjoyed it for two years. I went there and played and it was a good football club. I then went to Doncaster and had a couple of injuries. I had quite a bad knee injury, which they said I should have stopped playing on, really, but me being me, I wouldn't listen.

"I tried to get fit and I did – I got as fit as I'd been for years and years. And then on my second day back, I was messing around on the training ground, obviously being excited that my knee was good, and I dived into a puddle and dislocated my shoulder. And that more or less ended my career.

"I had four pins put in my shoulder through diving in a puddle. That was the end of the professional game, so I moved back to my house in Suffolk that I had from when I was at Ipswich. My knee was good and my shoulder got better over time and I still had an urge – I missed the day-to-day stuff of being involved in football, so I looked to play part time.

"A friend from Ipswich, Fabian Wilnis, suggested Needham Market. I drove past this club every morning on my way to Ipswich and I didn't know it existed. So I came down and trained, and they had a young manager and a young team at the time. And I thought, 'Yeah, I'll be a part of that'. I wanted to be part of something that could potentially kick on and do well.

"I came down and trained Tuesday and Thursday evenings and played Saturdays, which, at the time, without sounding too big-headed, players who had played in the Premier League didn't play at this level. So, at first, there were a few raised eyebrows on why I was doing it and what I was going to be like, but I'm still at this football club.

"I give everything like I did in any match, because as a footballer I had a half decent left foot, but I was limited, so I had to work harder. So even if I did that now and played a five-a-side game with the boys upstairs, I'd always work hard.

"This is my third season here now, I'm still enjoying it and I run the academy. I'm enjoying seeing the boys develop and trying to help them and give them a little bit of the experience I've been given over the years off all the good managers I've had.

"One of the lads has just been signed by Ipswich and it gives me a lot. It's not as good as playing football, nothing ever will be – certainly at a club like Man City – but it's probably the second best thing.

"I thought I was going to play football forever. It sounds bizarre now and even me saying it makes me wonder what I was thinking. You just don't think it's ever going to end, you just don't see it stopping right up until the day it does."

Coaching is certainly a role he's been able to adapt well to. In August 2013, he received a phone call to become the assistant manager of Northern Ireland's Under-21 squad.

"It came out of the blue," he says, "I went

"I would never have said that I'd have coached and if you ask any people that know me being the joker that I was, they'd probably say Kevin Horlock would never be a coach – especially with all the messing around and the not listening to coaches I did."

away and did the A-Licence in Ireland and obviously I'd played international football for them. A lad I used to play with, Steve Robinson, is the manager of the Under-21s and also an assessor on the coaching course.

"He just said to me that a position with the Under-21s might become available on a part time basis and asked if I'd be interested. I said, providing my day-to-day job at Needham Market wasn't going to be affected, then of course I would. The lad who had been doing it got a job with Cardiff and he [Robinson] rang me almost as soon as I got back. I met him in London and agreed to get involved.

"I would never have said that I'd have coached and if you ask any people that know me being the joker that I was, they'd probably say Kevin Horlock would never be a coach – especially with all the messing around and the not listening to coaches I did.

"But I enjoy it and I think I'm half decent at it."

7 MICHAEL BROWN

Starting in midfield at Wembley for Manchester City in 1999 was a Hartlepool-born product of the club's youth system. Michael Brown was promoted to the first team in the mid-'90s, following a successful campaign as the youth team captain. It meant he was involved in the 1995-96 preseason with the main squad, and he went on to make his debut in the August of that year.

And it was a very eventful debut at that. He joined the action in place of Steve Lomas during the second half of a 1-0 defeat to QPR at Loftus Road. He had been getting stuck in and showing the right attitude for a youngster breaking into the first team, but with just a few minutes to go, he found himself chasing Rangers' Andy Impey – who was bearing down on goal. Brown tugged his shirt to stop him and, despite there being a covering defender, the youngster was shown a straight red card by referee Paul Danson.

"I went on and I was there ten minutes," Brown recalls, "I was running round and trying hard, as you do when you're 17. We were a goal down and Impey just ran past me, so I tugged his shirt as he was heading towards goal. The ref thought I was the last man, but – I remember clearly – Alan Kernaghan was there, but those days when you got sent off there were no replays.

"It was from the highest moment to the lowest very, very quickly. I think that put me in good stead for my career, really. It taught me the highs and lows of football quite quickly! You have to kind of take it in your stride."

Brown was always likely to become a professional footballer given his application and attitude on the pitch. Even as a youngster, he could never be accused of shirking a challenge or not giving his all. He remembers the decision to join the Blues: "I'd been to a lot of clubs and I'd been offered a few places.

"Every school holiday, I'd go to a different place and Manchester City

CITY CAREER STATS
Apps: 109 (27 sub)
Goals: 4
Signed: July 1994
Left: December 1999
Debut: QPR (a), 1995
Result: 1-0 defeat

was one of the last ones I visited," he says. "I just felt like they didn't oversell it. They didn't try to say, 'This is the best place for you'. Terry Farrell was the guy in charge back then and it just seemed right. They just treated me and my dad right, they weren't throwing things at me or anything like that, it was just very straight down the line.

"I looked at the amount of players that had had a chance and had come through at City and it was a fantastic record, so I decided to go with it. They offered me a six-year contract when I was 14 – there was no money mentioned, it was just a matter of being with the club for that amount of time. It was about giving me a chance to be there for a length of time to prove myself.

"I had a good year for the youth team," he says, "I played up front, dropping into midfield a little bit. We'd done well in the youth cup and I'd managed to score a few goals. It was just great at Platt Lane on that pitch on the corner [of Platt Lane and Yew Tree Road] and we used to have some big days on Saturday mornings.

"There was a lot of change in managers," he continues, thinking about the level of stability at the club at the time, "I first went in under Peter Reid and then it changed quite quickly. At the start of that season [1995-96] Alan Ball had taken over, Terry Darracott was the coach – he was great with me and brought me through.

"When he went, Neil McNab came in and he pushed me very quickly. He would tell me where I was going wrong and where I needed to improve, and he pushed me quite hard to Alan Ball. The first team didn't start really well and I sort of skipped the reserves – I didn't really play a reserve team game.

"I found myself on the bench for the game at QPR and that's where it all started."

Brown's debut season in the first team didn't end well for the club. City finished 18th in the Premier League, level on points with both Southampton and Coventry, but with a worse goal difference. Looking

> "I went on and I was there ten minutes. [Andy] Impey just ran past me, so I tugged his shirt as he was heading towards goal. The ref thought I was the last man, but Alan Kernaghan was there, but those days when you got sent off there were no replays."

back now, the midfielder is philosophical about his first year in the team.

"I think you just look back and think how your career could have gone if you'd stayed up," he says. "It did knock us. It took me a while to get back to the Premier League. It definitely hinders you, but I think it teaches you to become headstrong. It teaches you the game – that it's a lot more than just going to training, or just a few skills, and that it's about mentality."

During the calendar year 1996, the Blues went through five managers – be it caretaker or permanent appointments. Following Alan Ball's resignation in the August, Asa Hartford took temporary charge until chairman Francis Lee appointed his new man. However, Steve Coppell lasted just 33 days before resigning himself due to the stress of the job. Phil Neal took the reins as caretaker until Frank Clark was given the position at the end of December.

Brown says that, in situations like the club was in at the time, the players have to adapt and just get on with the job. "I learnt very quickly," he says, "leaving City at the age of 21, I think I'd had ten managers and I think on my career now I'm on about 26! When a new man comes in, people are very similar so they just slightly tweak things. I think I can read situations very quickly now, and I read how and where things are heading."

As Brown began to become more involved with the first team and managers changed, the club started sliding towards its eventual relegation to the third tier in 1998.

"If I'm not mistaken," Brown remembers, "I think I'd done okay the season before. I think I got player of the year when we were in the old First Division. We were struggling, Joe Royle came in and we were relegated. It was a strange, strange situation that we managed to find ourselves in being such a massive club in the old Second Division.

"At the start of preseason, Joe Royle brought in a few players and I found myself not really being involved," Brown continues, "being a young lad coming from playing in the Premier League it was a bit of a shock to the system. It was difficult not starting the season.

"I just remember Joe Royle pulling me in and telling me, 'You've not been playing, you're going to Hull', who were Division Three at the time. So I said, 'Why haven't I been playing here?' So Joe said, 'They're [the other players] doing a better job and I want them to play, so I want you to go to Hull.'

"At that point, I looked at him and said, 'I'm not going to Hull, I'm going to stay here.' It was a big turning point in my career, because I just wonder where my career would have gone if I'd moved and just

"I'm from Hartlepool so to score against Darlington at any point is always a classic! It was in the early rounds [of the FA Cup]. All I remember is just mazing through!"

gone for it. I stuck to my guns.

"I got on well with the fans then and there was a pressure for the manager to put me back in. Come November or December, I came back in and we did well. I think we went almost unbeaten until the end of the season, so it worked out well that I came back in and we had a successful time.

"Once we got on a roll, you just knew we were going to the play-offs," he says. It's a sentiment that was echoed by a few of the players of that era that, even though City hit form around Christmas time, the start to the season had been so bad that it meant the Blues missed out on automatic promotion.

One of the key moments that helped Brown force his way back into the first team came in the FA Cup – a tournament that City had had to enter from the first round rather than the third, due to their status in the English league. The Blues had eased past Halifax in their first game, but had stumbled to a 1-1 draw away to Darlington in the second. The replay at Maine Road was into extra time when the deciding goal was scored – coming from Brown in an eventual 1-0 win.

"I scored one of my better goals," Brown says about that game. When I ask if he remembers it, he laughs. "I do, because I'm from Hartlepool so to score against Darlington at any point is always a classic! It was the early rounds so it'd have been around November time, so obviously I was only playing because it was the cup. I did well and found myself back in the team.

"All I remember is just mazing through!"

What Brown says does something of a disservice to his goal. With the game poised at 0-0, Gareth Taylor volleyed a cross from the right at goal, but it was blocked by one of the defenders. Brown picked up the loose ball on the edge of the box and carried it, as a wall of red Darlington shirts raced out towards him. He skipped past two challenges and dashed in-between two of the others to go one-on-one with the goalkeeper. There, the Blues' number seven took it around the slide challenge from the keeper, before turning and slotting the ball into the unguarded goal.

"Just mazing through" makes it sound like a simple strike!

He begins to talk about the 1998-99 campaign as a whole, specifically what he remembers as one of the turning points of the winter. "It was a very strange season," he says, "we went to Wrexham and were still only about 12th at this point. It was Boxing Day and I was struggling with a heavy cold, I was dying!

"We managed to hang in there. We were terrible, but we managed to nick it 1-0. It was only years later that I heard a rumour that Joe Royle would have been sacked had we lost that game. We nicked through and managed to crack on and get to Wembley."

Brown started the Play-Off Final with Gillingham, as he had for all of the games in the build-up to the match throughout the first five months of 1999. Having played his way into the team, he had become a mainstay in a midfield that was helping the Blues climb the table.

"There was massive hype because it looked like we were clear favourites," he says, thinking back to the morning of the Play-Off Final, "though we only just scraped through the two legs with Wigan, really. But I felt confident that morning and I felt like we had a good enough team to win.

"We had a good bunch of players and momentum on our side," he continues, "and obviously the support of the fans – we knew that wasn't going to be a problem. But it was almost the day of the underdog, as Gillingham came and played really well.

"I've met a few of the lads from that team along the way in my career," he says, with a little hint of a smile arriving on his face, "they weren't happy! How we won that game, I'll never know."

Brown left the action before the goalscoring mayhem began, being replaced just after the hour mark. Ian Bishop took the midfielder's place in the team in the 61st minute, as Joe Royle tried to freshen things up a little.

"It was strange," he says, "we were kind of neck and neck and Joe and Willie thought, 'We've got to go and win it'. So they made attacking changes and went for it. Then in the final ten minutes we found ourselves 2-0 down, so sometimes you have to be careful what you wish for!

"Willie Donachie, though, never knew when he was beaten. He tried to instil into the players that you keep going and going, and on that day he wasn't wrong. It came off for him, the players and the team. You're never beaten until the final whistle.

"It was my first time at Wembley and I'd always wanted to play there since I was a little boy. It was a strange day and I think some City fans forget those days now. You go back now and see that some fans see the Premier League and being Champions.

"But I think a lot of City fans would remember what they've been through and I think that's why it's such a unique story how they got back and then went on to win the Premier League. It's probably only City that could do it – and that's what City was."

Some would argue that's what City *still* is and the more that 'Typical City' seems to be a thing of the past, the more it returns to the club.

I asked Brown what it was like to still be a relatively young lad in such an important game. His reply says all you need to know about the instability at the Blues at that time: "I think from such a young age – at 16 or 17 – and going through manager changes, going up and going down through the leagues... it was just another day at City.

"It was great, all the ups and downs, and it taught me a lot," he continues, "but it was never straightforward."

Despite playing an integral part of City's turn in fortune in the 1998-99 season and in getting the Blues to the Play-Off Final, Brown was something of a bit-part player the following year. In the end, he moved to Sheffield United, initially on loan before making the switch permanently.

"It was the start of the next season," Brown says, explaining how the move came about, "I'm not a right midfielder and I've gone in for preseason and Joe was playing me in right midfield, so I half smelt a rat that I wasn't going to be near the pitch.

> "It was a bit of fate. I was a young lad, different to what I am now, and as a young lad I was still growing up and developing and I might have been a bit cheeky."

"The first game came and I was left out. So it started like the season before, with the manager not using me and thinking that everyone else could do a better job, which was Joe's right.

"I felt a bit disappointed, really, because I felt I'd heavily done my part and deserved to start the next season to see how I could do then," he continues, "and then if I didn't perform, I'd expect to be left out. But I didn't get that chance.

"Eventually, the team were doing ok and I took a loan to Portsmouth with Alan Ball again. But he was sacked quite quickly and I came back and went straight to Sheffield United. Neil Warnock needed players and he said that he had no money, but that if I went and was playing, I'd get a move from there.

"I started playing and playing well, and he [Warnock] said, 'I'd love to keep you, but I don't know with regards to money.' The club wanted £400,000, but Neil Warnock said he'd try and get me for £375,000.

"Joe Royle wanted to make sure I couldn't play against City the following week, but Neil Warnock told him the deal was off. In the end, Joe took the offer and then Sheffield United won 1-0 at Bramall Lane the week later and I scored the goal.

"It was a bit of fate," he says, "I was a young lad, different to what I am now, and as a young lad I was still growing up and developing and I might have been a bit cheeky. But I think I'd done well for City over the years, especially as a 17-year-old, and I think it was a shame I had to leave, but I've been to some fantastic clubs and I'm glad I've played for different clubs.

"I think it's quite obvious that I could have done a job for City for the next couple of years, though," he says, "but it was just one manager's choice. I just think Joe didn't want to use me until he was in such a situation where he was 12th in the Second Division and I think I just came in at the right time and we won the games.

"I felt like I could have played more games and we don't know what would have gone on, but I can't moan about the career I've had – I've had a good career."

From being on the right end of a Manchester City comeback – albeit briefly – Brown found himself on the wrong end of one some years later. By this stage in his career, he'd moved to Tottenham, who were being managed by David Pleat. City, now under the stewardship of Kevin Keegan and struggling in the Premier League, were drawn against Spurs in the FA Cup.

Following a 1-1 draw at Eastlands, the Blues travelled to White Hart Lane for the replay, having won one game (in the previous round of the FA Cup) in their last 16 matches in all competitions. At half time, the home side were winning 3-0 and City youngster Joey Barton was shown a second yellow card for something he said to the referee during the break. They were virtually out of the tie.

A man down and three goals down, somehow the Blues went on to win 4-3 – with goals from Sylvain Distin, Paul Bosvelt, Shaun Wright-Phillips and Jon Macken.

"Amazing game," Brown says, "we were 3-0 up and Joey had been mouthing at the referee at half time and got sent off. He was getting frustrated and had left a bit on someone and the referee didn't like it. He didn't like getting beat – nobody does.

"But with the talented players City had then, they came out in the second half on the front foot and we came out slightly sloppily, and it was 3-1 quite quickly. Then it snowballed and you knew it was coming, but you couldn't do anything about it!

"You look back and laugh now and just think, 'How did that happen?' But that's football and that's City. It's never straightforward."

The discussion heads towards comebacks with the Blues – against Gillingham in 1999, against Tottenham in 2004, against QPR in 2012 – and that last one makes Brown wonder if the club is too far removed today of what it was when he left. "It's a great club, but I think it's lost a bit of that homely feel it used to have. City was a properly homely club, where everybody knew everybody.

> "...they came out in the second half on the front foot and we came out slightly sloppily, and it was 3-1 quite quickly. Then it snowballed and you knew it was coming, but you couldn't do anything about it!"

"It's gone on to big things and maybe you have to sacrifice some of that to take it to the level they're at now," he says, "but it's good to see."

At the time of doing the interview in the autumn of 2013, Brown had just finished training at Leeds, where he had been playing since 2011. He'd played against City for the Elland Road club in the 2012-13 FA Cup, where Roberto Mancini's Blues powered into the next round with a 4-0 win.

"It was good to go back to City because you start to think that, all the teams you've played for or been involved with, as each season goes on, the less opportunities you're going to get to go back to them clubs. We played Tottenham and then City, so that was great.

"At 37, your opportunities get less and less," he says, "I'm happy to still be playing and I just want to keep playing my football – I know there's not long left and I'm at another big club – like City – at Leeds. We're still trying to get back into the Premier League, as City did, and if we do it, I imagine it could just be the same. It could just roll on."

For Brown personally, he says he's not sure what he wants to do when he retires. "I just want to keep playing," he says, "I don't mind dropping down, but we'll see how it goes. I'll try and get to 40. That's my aim.

"I've played in all the leagues throughout my career, so maybe I'll do it again at the end of my career."

The City squad and coaching staff celebrate their Play-Off Final win *(top)*; Nicky Weaver calls his team forward to begin the celebrations after his final penalty save *(bottom left)*; Terry Cooke slides in for the ball on Gillingham's Nicky Southall *(bottom right)*.

Manager Joe Royle shows his relief at winning the game *(top left)*; Nicky Weaver won't let the trophy out of his grasp after the match *(top right)*; The City squad link arms during penalties, something Ian Bishop (fourth from the left) claims to have invented *(bottom)*.

Paul Dickov (number 9, centre) is mobbed after his equaliser with just seconds of the game remaining *(top)*; Skipper Andy Morrison lifts the play-off trophy *(bottom left)*; Nicky Weaver's mad run is brought to an abrupt end by his captain *(bottom right)*.

Gerard Wiekens (centre) sticks tight to striker Carl Asaba, as Gillingham attack *(top)*; Nicky Weaver punches a ball into City's box clear *(bottom)*.

Nicky Weaver saves the first Gillingham penalty to give City the advantage in the shoot-out *(top)*; Kevin Horlock *(bottom left)* and Richard Edghill *(bottom right)* celebrate converting their spot-kicks (penalties one and four) in front of the City supporters.

City players defend a high ball into the box *(top)*; Kevin Horlock (centre) celebrates after Gillingham's fourth penalty is saved *(bottom)*.

8 JEFF WHITLEY

Of all the players in the 1999 Play-Off Final squad, Jeff Whitley's story is possibly the most hard-hitting. Having broken into the first team at City, the midfielder never got the support he needed off the football pitch and it could have had disastrous consequences. While in the public eye he was a young professional footballer having a good time, what wasn't known was that he was an alcoholic and would, in the latter stages of his career, become addicted to cocaine.

CITY CAREER STATS

Apps: 141 (30 sub)
Goals: 8

Signed: February 1996
Left: March 2003

Debut: Barnsley (h), 1996
Result: 2-1 defeat

He earned his place in the Manchester City first team squad in 1996. "It came as quite a shock," he says when I ask about when he found out he would be in the team, "players at the time were being bled in slowly and I was sat next to Lee Crooks at the time – I had no inkling I was going to be in the squad. It was so unexpected.

"When the team was named, it took me a while to take it in," he continues, "then all the lads were coming over and saying things like, 'All the best, Jeff!' and then a bit of fear kicked in. I had to go and just take a few minutes – it was quite a nerve-racking experience.

"I didn't realise how big the Kippax actually was, not until I went out of the tunnel. It was only then that I saw it for the first time and it was quite unbelievable."

Whitley's first goal for the club came in his 16th senior game – which wasn't bad for a midfielder who, by his own admission, didn't rank shooting as one of his major assets – after he replaced Neil Heaney in a 3-2 win over Bradford. It was the winning goal, after the Bantams had come from 2-0 down to pull level.

The Zambian-born Northern Ireland international netted his second goal of his career against the same side, this time in the away fixture the following season. It was an eventful game for Whitley, who, after giving the Blues the lead at Valley Parade in March 1998, was sent off for dissent in the closing stages of a 2-1 defeat.

By this stage, Whitley was onto his third City manager, despite only having been a first team player for two seasons. Alan Ball had resigned right at the beginning of the midfielder's debut season, with Frank Clark taking up the reins. When he was sacked in February 1998, Joe Royle came in and was tasked with reducing the wage bill as well as keeping the team in Division One.

Whitley's future at City might have looked in jeopardy when he was loaned to Wrexham at the start of 1999 – midway through the club's only season in the third tier. But, when he returned in the March, he played his way back into the team and earned himself a starting position for the Play-Off Final.

"I got up on the morning [of the game] and was still feeling like, 'Wow, are we really going to be playing at Wembley?' because it was a bit of a dream, really," he says when I ask how he was feeling pre-match and whether he was anxious, "it's a huge stadium and it's got a lot of history, so it was quite nervy.

"But I was very nervous when we eventually walked into the stadium," he continues, "usually, we were trying to have a bit of light banter – trying to keep your mind off the game because if that's all you think about you can put yourself under some real pressure."

Whitley did take part in one activity the day before the game that helped to relieve some tension in the camp. As the squad was returning to the hotel after a walk, the heavens opened and there was a torrential downpour. Everybody dashed for cover, but for the midfielder and his international teammate Kevin Horlock.

A competition began: whoever took shelter first was the loser.

When I remind him of the incident, he laughs. "Kev was a great character in the dressing room," he says, "he was phenomenal and a joy to be around. He was a very funny guy. I don't know who came up with the idea [of staying out in the rain], but things like that just helped people to bond.

"I couldn't tell you who won," he adds, "I think we actually walked in together, hugging each other. I can't remember exactly."

I can't help but jump in here as he's trying to remember what happened and give Horlock's version of events: "Kev told me that you went in first," I say and instantly he laughs in response.

"Oh, he would say that!" he replies amongst the laughter. "He would say that, that's him all over! I'm pretty sure we went in together, hugging each other and saying, 'What are we doing out here?'"

It was all about relieving pressure. Whitley explains to me that one of the biggest things for the squad for that game was keeping a lid on the nerves and making sure the atmosphere remained light.

"When you're on your way to games," he says, "you can start to play the game in your head – you want to play a good game, you want to have a good first touch, all those sorts of things. But because you're not there yet, I always tried to keep it light and just talk to the lads. You can really start to feel nervous.

"On the drive up to the stadium, I was just trying to soak it all in and just be in the moment, really. When we got off the coach, I remember walking into the stadium and dropping our stuff off, before walking out onto the pitch through the tunnel. I thought Maine Road was big, but Wembley was a totally different kettle of fish."

One of the common themes throughout the interviews for this book has been the size of the pitch. Some of the players were tired because of it, some found it difficult to keep going because they felt it was wet and heavy – but it affected Whitley, who played 120 minutes on the surface, in a completely different way.

"I remember going into extra time and I was feeling exhausted, but also I was absolutely starving," he says, "and we didn't have any Jaffa Cakes or anything like that. You see some players run off and grab something, have a little bite, and I could really have done with an energy boost going into extra time. I was getting a sickly feeling because I was so hungry and I was just trying to get rid of that by drinking fluids.

"I remember going into extra time and I was feeling exhausted, but also I was absolutely starving and we didn't have any Jaffa Cakes or anything like that. I was getting a sickly feeling because I was so hungry..."

"The rest of it was just willpower," he says, "until the body starts cramping up, you just have to keep going. I didn't really feel like the pitch was heavy; it was well maintained and a joy to play on – most footballers will tell you they like it with a little bit of zip on when it's wet. It also means you can put some sliding tackles in without the skin coming off!

"But when we'd won the penalties, I remember going into the dressing room, congratulating Dicky [Paul Dickov] and then diving straight in the food! It was a great occasion to play at the old Wembley before it was demolished and to win the way we did probably made it even more special."

With Whitley desperate for food, he might have felt as though he was going to get something to eat when there was about three minutes to play. Goals from Carl Asaba and Robert Taylor had left the Blues 2-0 down and, with not long left, it looked like it was all over.

"I remember looking at the clock and thinking that there were about three or four minutes left," he says, "I felt like we'd got that far that we couldn't die out then, even though there was only a few minutes to go.

"We also had a really good squad of players," he continues, "I can't remember being in a team like that. When we were promoted and promoted again, we had a phenomenal squad – we trained hard and we had a good laugh off the field as well. In a lot of games – just like with Gillingham – we fought hard together and we fought to the end. Luckily, it went our way."

One of the key moments in the match that Whitley was involved in came in the second half of extra time. With six minutes to go before full time, City might have found themselves behind once again had the referee penalised the Blues' midfielder for handball. Gillingham's John Hodge had got to the byline on the left side of the box and tried to cut the ball back. Whitley, sliding it, managed to get it behind for a corner, but it was with his trailing arm – and City were lucky.

"I think it was [handball]," he says, "I've not intentionally gone to handball it, but it has hit my hand and it could have been another turning point. It happened so quickly – sometimes you're not conscious of wanting to stay on your feet, but you want to just stop the ball and you want to dive in and win that tackle. But decisions like that have been given in certain games."

We begin to talk about the penalty shootout. The old cliché is that it's a 'lottery', which is perhaps an over-egged way of saying that it's simply the luck of the draw whether a goalkeeper guesses the right way or whether the usually reliable striker can hit the target. Whitley says that he had the utmost respect for those who volunteered to take kicks.

"I don't think at that point I could have even kicked another ball," he says, "I was so, so exhausted. All credit to the lads that actually got up and took the penalties and to get up and take them at that stage of the game is brave. I know how much pressure there is. I didn't take one at Wembley, but I took one at Sunderland [in a Play-Off Semi Final with Crystal Palace in 2004] and I ended up missing."

Whitley says it was also a benefit for the Blues to have taken their penalties in front of the City fans. The commentator on the VHS season review described it as 'a wall of noise' when Gillingham's first taker, Paul Smith, ran up to strike his spot-kick. It must have played a part in three of the Gills players missing. "It was good also because we didn't have far to run – except when Weaver went on his mad run around the ground! I soon got a burst of energy, but I think I nearly cramped up then!"

Whitley was also part of the City team to win promotion at Ewood Park a year later. The visitors were pummelled for the first half and were a goal down needing to draw, and the midfielder remembers it well: "We'd been absolutely battered for about an hour. But it was just meant to be. They hit the bar and the post about five times, but then our goals just came."

The midfielder was a regular in the City side that played in the Premier League the following season, but everything changed for him following the club's relegation back to Division One. With Joe Royle being replaced by Kevin Keegan in the manager's dugout, the entire squad was given a clean slate. This meant that, despite Whitley's regular appearances, he was effectively playing for his place in the side.

He started Keegan's tenure on the bench against Watford, coming on for the final 13 minutes of the 3-0 home win. He was named as a substitute for City's trip to Norwich in the second match of the season and both joined and departed the action sooner than he would have been expecting. After 20 minutes he replaced the injured Eyal Berkovic, but was stretchered off less than an hour later.

"I broke my leg," he remembers, "and it was

"It was all about mental toughness and keeping yourself positive. I didn't. I did all the wrong things to cheer myself up a bit. I went out a lot. Loads of people were telling me to calm down..."

very tough. I'd never had a long injury like that throughout my career and I didn't know how to deal with it. If I knew then what I know now, I'd have spoken to players who had suffered long injuries and found out how they dealt with it.

"It was all about mental toughness and keeping yourself positive," he says. "I didn't. I did all the wrong things to cheer myself up a bit. I went out a lot. Loads of people were telling me to calm down and Kevin Keegan had several words with me before he'd had enough.

"I came back and went on loan to Notts County and had a good time there. I helped to save them from relegation and it was a wonderful time, but then I came back [to City] and just wasn't in his [Keegan's] plans. A lot of that was to do with my antics off the field, which I feel the clubs I played for could have done a little bit more to help me with. It's alright telling someone to stop drinking and stop partying... give them a solution and they might."

I ask Whitley how often he was going out drinking. "It varied," he replies, "I could have stayed in for weeks on end, but then it started off on a Saturday and [would] sometimes roll into a Sunday. I say 'sometimes' but it became quite a regular thing on a Sunday.

"Before long, it was Monday, Tuesday, Wednesday. I'd stay off it on Thursday and Friday, and then play on Saturday. And then the longer it went on, it would carry on into the Thursday and Friday, even before big games.

"I didn't know what addiction was and I didn't know how to deal with it. I'm sure if you ask anybody what an addict is or to describe an addict or ask how they deal with

"I could have stayed in for weeks on end, but then it started off on a Saturday and sometimes roll into a Sunday... Before long, it was Monday, Tuesday, Wednesday. I'd stay off it on Thursday and Friday and then play on Saturday."

their addictions, I don't think there'll be many people who would be able to answer. Or they would think of somebody like a tramp on a park bench or something like that, drinking his bottle of cider. As it happens, you can be addicted to anything – and if you don't deal with it and don't understand it, it will either kill you or it will ruin your life.

"My addiction got hold of me and ruined my life," he continues, "but I don't blame anybody for that. I don't blame City, I don't blame my friends – people often say, 'It must be the amount of money you had', but there are addicts out there who didn't have anywhere near as much money as I had, but they're still addicts.

"It's not just drink and drugs," he continues, "there's so many things people can chuck to – there are people who are workaholics who don't see their families or there are kids who are up until three or four in the morning playing computer games."

Whitley tells me it can be very difficult for footballers that suffer from an addiction. Not that he's looking for sympathy – far from it, he tells me he's never been happier – but the general public can be very unsympathetic: "People can say, 'He had his chance' or, 'We told him numerous times to stop drinking and to stop going out', but I never understood what an addict was or how an addict behaved – if I did, I might have stopped.

"I'm not saying it would have saved me," he says, "but I think there are footballers out there now who will be slipping through the net because they've got unsolved issues. My issues were things that caught up with me later on in life that I didn't know how to deal with – losing my parents at a young age, I'd never seen two people connect and have a healthy relationship. I never learnt the values of life and what was important; I didn't know I had a massive ego and low self-esteem.

"I think there are footballers out there now who will be slipping through the net because they've got unsolved issues. My issues were things that caught up with me later on in life that I didn't know how to deal with..."

"These were all things I had to work on to be able to love the person I am today and understand the person I am today. And I mean that in a non-egotistical manner. There were times when I was playing football and people who say, 'You're doing a job that you love', but if you're not happy in yourself then you're not going to love what you're doing and you're not going to be grateful for what you've got.

"It's like that with any job – regardless of whether it's football," he continues. "If you're not happy within yourself, you're not going to go into any job raring to go because your head's not there. My head wasn't there for years."

Whitley explains that he was using drink and drugs to escape from how he was feeling. "It was a release from this empty hole that I was feeling inside," he says, "it got filled with alcohol, women, buying things, a cocktail of different drugs... and it got rid of it for a little while.

"There was a coach who had known me for a long, long time who said he thought I'd just fallen out of love with the game," he says, "he didn't know I was a chronic alcoholic and I was addicted to cocaine."

I ask the former midfielder when he realised he had a problem and he takes a moment to think about it. "I sort of already knew I had a problem, but I didn't know how to deal with it. Going into big games and knowing that the week before you've not prepared – you don't need to be Einstein to realise you've not prepared for a game.

"But I couldn't stop," he says. "I couldn't stop."

He says he hopes people can relate to what he's saying. "An alcoholic isn't somebody who goes home and has a drink. There are people that have to leave work and go to the pub because they've had a stressful day. They'll go and have two pints – or three, or four, or five – and then they'll go home, knowing that they're over the limit. If they have to do that every day in order to chill out, I would say that's a problem.

"I know now that I'm allergic to it," he continues, "I know that once I put a drink into my system, the mental craving for me doubles. And it does that every time I put another drink into my system – so I might have all intentions of going home after two or three drinks, but I think, 'I'll just have one more because I'm with the lads.'

"Then I start lying to my missus and before I know it I've had seven or eight. And I used to do that so many times," he says, "so many times. There were loads of different scenarios.

"I got to a point where I was running out of money. I was physically dying. Without going into too much detail of my physical presence, I was coughing up and throwing up blood – and that was only minor, I can't go into too much detail. Towards the end, I would only go to sleep when my body shut down.

"I would go for days or weeks without sleeping.

"I'd had enough and I'd fallen out of love with myself," he says, "and I was praying to die. I was missing my parents. It was such a dark and lonely place that you don't want to share with anybody and you isolate – it was complete and total isolation. And there was only me that could have got to that point and say that I needed help.

"I was physically dying... I was coughing up and throwing up blood... Towards the end, I would only go to sleep when my body shut down."

"All the clubs I played at knew that I had a drink problem."

Whitley tells me that it was around this time that his daughter was born, too. He went into rehab three days later. He tells me that making the call was one of the hardest things he's ever done.

"They basically strip you down," he says, "right down to your skeleton and then rebuild you to try and help you understand the person that you are. I didn't know who I was – that was the scary thing. I was 28 or 29 years old and I didn't know who I was.

"Nobody likes being told the choices they're making or the way they're living their life isn't right," he continues, "they point out blind spots – things that you don't know you're doing, but that other people can see you're doing. I had a lot of blind spots.

"Hey, I'm not at all perfect," he says, "but what I do have today is that I'm truly happy in myself and that was something I couldn't find when I was playing football. Don't get me wrong – I had some great times when I was playing, but a lot of people look at footballers and think it's a great life and they've got everything and it's not quite like that.

"There are a lot of lonely players out there. I was nowhere near in the limelight that some of the players are. If you're famous and can't walk out of your front door or sit in a restaurant without attention and if you can't deal with that, then you'll never go out."

Whitley is very open about his experiences with addiction and that's something he hopes will help others who have suffered or are suffering with similar issues. "I want people to know that, whatever you're going through in life, there is a solution.

"I got into Alcoholics Anonymous, I got into Narcotics Anonymous, into Cocaine Anonymous – these are different fellowships that I go to on a regular basis. I know I cannot stay off drink and drugs by myself. I have to stay in contact with other addicts who understand me and understand where my head is. And when I am struggling I'm able to pick up the phone and say, 'Hey, I'm struggling, can I come and see you?' I stay clean and sober because of people I try and help and they help me.

"I'll never shut the door on my past and how bad it was when I think about it," he says, "and I don't want to go there today. I can't say I'm never going to drink again or I'm never going to use drugs again – I live on a daily basis. Today, I don't want to drink and I don't want to use.

"Whenever I'm feeling down, I look at my 'gratitude list'," he says, "I look at it and think, 'Hey – what do I have to be miserable about? I've got a roof over my head. I've got food in the cupboard. I've got a beautiful family and a missus that I totally respect and love.'

"I'm a happier person today. I don't have to hide anything. I'm not waiting on a phone call from somebody giving me grief because I've been doing the wrong thing or I've been out and too drunk to remember. I have a nice life – I don't have what I thought would bring happiness and all the materialistic things, but I realise today that that's just not important."

When I first interviewed the former midfielder, he was working with Mick McCarthy at Wolves to help their youngsters understand what addiction was and to provide a platform for them to speak about how they were feeling. He was offering the players support – speaking from his own experiences of the lies he used to tell or the behaviours he used to exhibit when he was hiding how he was really feeling.

He told me that it was all about trying to educate the youngsters so that they weren't affected when they were older. However, the scheme Whitley was working with stopped when the manager at Molineux was sacked in 2012.

He's disappointed that the meetings were stopped, but he hopes it's something he can do in the future: "I think it could be a full time job, having mentors in football clubs and having someone who is able to see the lads on a daily basis and try and understand them," he says, "I think that's one thing that football's lacking. It's all about the football – if you can play, great, but if you can't, it's see you later. And it's not really bothered about what's going on in the brain, especially in the brains of the younger lads.

"If you show any sign of weakness, people jump on you," he says, talking about the levels of pressure in football, "I'd love to see that totally kicked out of the game and have lads speak freely about how they're feeling."

Whitley now works at an independent used car retailer in Stockport and has just passed his UEFA B-Licence. He tells me that he's hoping to become a manager in the future, because "it's the next best thing" to playing.

He also thinks that the way the club won the Premier League in 2012 showed him what the fans were feeling when he was on the pitch in 1999. "It was good to be on both sides," he says, "to actually be there when Aguero put that goal in, I've got to say... I was in tears that day. I was in pieces. I was just running like a madman, jumping on anybody!

"Obviously being at Wembley was an immense day for the players and the fans," he continues, "it was a long season. So being there as a player and then being there as a fan was truly emotional. People said that you couldn't have topped Wembley, but that Aguero goal was right up there.

"I'd have loved to have played in that squad!"

9 PAUL DICKOV
Striker

Before the match at Wembley, the headlines were being prepared already for one particular story that was eclipsed by the dramatic nature of the ending to the game. City's number nine that afternoon – Paul Dickov – had previously been a teammate of Gillingham's number one, Vince Bartram, when the two played at Arsenal.

Many newspaper column inches had been dedicated to this in the build-up. Dickov had been best man at Bartram's wedding, before Bartram later returned the favour for the striker. On the afternoon of the game, *The Sunday Mirror* opted for the headline 'May The Best Man Win' – and the chances are that title was printed a few more times across a few more publications that weekend.

In the end, the most dramatic moment of the tie came when Dickov placed City's equaliser past his old friend and into the top corner of Gillingham's net, with seconds of injury time remaining. Did the striker have mixed emotions about that goal?

"Absolutely not!" he says, "I still remind Vince about it now!

"The weird thing is that, just before Christmas time, me and Vince and our families were together and we'd actually spoken about, if it came down to the play-offs, what it would be like playing against each other. And I just said to him that it wouldn't affect me in the slightest! If anything, it makes you more determined to get one over your mate.

"I know Vince still takes stick now saying that he did me a favour by pulling his hand out of the way. But I still see him a lot and he's a very good friend."

CITY CAREER STATS
Apps: 199 (68 sub)
Goals: 41
Signed: August 1996, May 2006
Left: February 2002, June 2008
First Debut: Stoke (a), 1996
Result: 2-1 defeat
Second Debut: Chelsea (a), 2006
Result: 3-0 defeat

It's a moment that, in the years since the game, fans have watched over and over again, but a moment that Dickov tells me he doesn't remember much about: "It was one of them things that was instinctive," he says. "Even now when I look back and I see it and I see my celebration, it was nothing I could have done before or done afterwards or re-enacted. It was just passion, ecstasy, relief...

"I just think about the work I'd done on my finishing that season," he continues. "Before that, I think my finishing was a bit hit and miss, but I worked really hard that season on my first touch and hitting the target, and it all seemed to come together.

"But, as for the actual goal itself, I can't remember a lot about it."

The strike ended up being one of the most crucial in the club's history. Without it, questions will always be asked about where Manchester City would be today – though it would be difficult to say they would never have recovered, you could make a good case that they would never have been Premier League champions and FA Cup winners in the time since.

"It was a massive occasion for everyone connected to the club," Dickov says. "The build-up to the game, City fans queuing for God knows how long trying to get tickets... and, although it wasn't mentioned too much, the players knew that it was make or break time for the football club. It didn't have to be mentioned because we knew that if we didn't get promoted then the club could have been in serious shit, really.

"It was only really in the week after the game where certain things came out about how the club could have possibly gone bust or gone into administration, but in the weeks leading up to the game Joe [Royle] and David Bernstein kept that away from us. We knew it was important because Manchester City is a big club, but not to the extent that we found out afterwards."

Before the game, confidence in the camp had been high. Leading up to the play-offs, the Blues had been in sensational form – they had to be for the club to even get close to the automatic promotion spots after such a poor first half of the season.

"To go on the run we did and to actually get there was a fantastic achievement," Dickov says about the club leaping out of mid-table and into third for the end of the season. "We had the nerve-wracking games against Wigan in the semi-final, but we managed to scrape through."

Dickov actually had another honour in the build-up to the Play-Off Final that year, too. In the first of the two semi-finals, his second half equaliser was the final goal ever scored at Wigan's Springfield Park stadium, before the club moved to the JJB – now the DW – Stadium. That goal, however, balanced out a first-minute mix-up between Gerard Wiekens and Nicky Weaver, which allowed Stuart Barlow to open the scoring with virtually the first kick of the game.

I asked whether Wiekens was the first player to congratulate Dickov on his equaliser and the Scot laughs. "He was," he says, "but Gerard didn't have to thank me or apologise because he was outstanding that season. It was a really uncharacteristic mistake from him.

"Obviously we got back in it – we were probably unlucky not to win the game," he continues, "we took them back to Maine Road [in the second leg] and it was a really nervy night. Wigan were probably the better team, but the Goat did what the Goat does and shanked one in."

If that second leg against Wigan was nervy, then surely the build-up to the Play-Off Final would have had the striker feeling worse?

"Joe, to be fair to him, tried to treat it like any other away game we'd played," he continues, "it was a little bit different. We knew we were playing at Wembley and we knew the importance of the game, so there was a little bit of nerves. But I don't think that's a bad thing – and, on a personal note, if I wasn't nervous before a game, I'd worry a little bit.

"I remember when they scored their second goal, I crouched down on all fours and I could feel myself welling up. For me, getting beaten didn't come into my head once that week and the fact that we were 2-0 down with not very long to go at all was just devastating. But we had a lot of character in that team."

"...when they scored their second goal, I crouched down on all fours and I could feel myself welling up. For me, getting beaten didn't come into my head once that week..."

It could have been a completely different story, though. Shortly after Carl Asaba had opened the scoring, the ball broke kindly to Dickov just wide of the penalty spot, after Richard Edghill had driven it straight back into the box. With the score at 1-0, the striker got there first and managed to stretch to divert the ball towards goal. However, Bartram stuck out his foot and managed to get it in the way to block.

"I just remember missing... well, Vince saving the chance from me," the striker says. "It would have made a big difference and I just thought, 'I've got to get us out of this.' There was a belief among the team that there was only us who could change it. That was the character within the squad that took us from 12th and into the play-offs."

Things went from bad to worse with the second Gillingham goal, but hope was quickly restored: "Even when we went to 2-1, I can't remember once looking up to see how long was left," Dickov says, "I just had a feeling that once Kevin [Horlock] scored that we were going to do it. I remember looking at a couple of the Gillingham players' faces when Kevin scored the goal and we were going back for kick-off and they were shitting themselves. That filtered through to us all.

"It's easy to say it now, but I believed when we went back to take the kick-off that I had one more chance in me," he continues, "I just had a feeling that I was going to get one more chance before the end of the game. I didn't have time to think about it, but if I did I'd have probably have missed it, to tell you the truth!

"I couldn't repeat that [the knee-slide celebration] with the same passion as I did it then," he says, "it was just a moment of relief. And the noise that the fans made and that the players made when they were on top of me is something I'll always remember."

Having already spoken to Kevin Horlock by the time I'd travelled to Doncaster to speak to the former City striker, I had to ask him about what his ex-teammate had said. According to Horlock, Dickov had slipped and fallen flat on his face – but because of the celebrations nobody other than the striker and the midfielder knew about it.

Before I've even finished the question, Dickov's interrupted with a big grin on his face: "Funny," he says, "really funny." He tells the story, though I can't help but feel there's still a slight tinge of embarrassment in his voice at what happened.

"We ended up absolutely pissing ourselves laughing," he says. "I've been down on my knees and all the players have come over and Kev was the last one. As I've stood up, I've turned to throw my arms up to the crowd on my own, but I ended up spinning around, slipping and falling flat on my face. How the cameras haven't got it, I'll never know.

"It's something that me and Kev still laugh about now – he still winds me up all the time by saying that it was his goal that made me. And his goal does get forgotten about – he was a massive driving force behind us that season, so he can't say that whenever I talk about my Wembley goal, I don't mention him anymore!"

> "As I've stood up, I've turned to throw my arms up to the crowd on my own, but I ended up spinning around, slipping and falling flat on my face. How the cameras haven't got it, I'll never know."

However, the 95th minute equaliser wasn't where the drama ended for Dickov that afternoon. After securing extra time, City found it hard to break through Gillingham's defence and the additional 30 minutes was something of a non-event. The game went to penalties and – from hero to villain – the striker became the only one of the Blues to miss his kick. Not that he could have got much closer to scoring.

"I was feeling really confident," he says, "we'd been taking penalties in training since probably before the Wigan game. It was sod's law that I couldn't replicate what I did in training on a matchday because every single penalty that I took – and there must have been hundreds of them – went in that side netting.

"Even the big galoot Weaves still couldn't save it when I was telling him where I was going to put it," he continues, "I must have been the only one in training that didn't miss a penalty, but even when the ball hit the post I thought it was still going to go in.

"The worst thing about it was I've sent Vince the wrong way. He was going for a pie in the stadium because he'd gone the wrong way! Then for it to hit both posts, my heart just sunk.

"It just summed up the day. I must have gone through every emotion possible."

After a draining day, the squad travelled back to Manchester on the team bus. Celebrations were at a minimum – in fact, the club turned down an open top bus parade as they felt rescuing a third tier play-off final wasn't something the fans would want to fill the streets for, given the club's history of successes. But, the Dickov household did host a barbeque for the squad.

"I don't think I had much sleep that night," he says, "so we just carried on into the next day. The funniest story I can tell about it was Ian Bishop – who was a character – stayed in London with his family. He called me about 12 o'clock on the next day to find out how it was going when he was having some lunch somewhere near Kings Cross. Bish hated missing out on anything, so I told him all the boys were there and were all having a laugh – then about 4

> "...we'd been taking penalties in training since probably before the Wigan game. It was sod's law that I couldn't replicate what I did in training on a matchday because every single penalty I took went in that side netting."

o'clock my front door went and it was Bish. He'd left his family, gone straight to Kings Cross, jumped on a train and ended up at my house."

City went from strength to strength following that victory at Wembley. Almost a year later, the Blues had the chance to bounce back to the Premier League, heading into the final day of the 1999-2000 season at Blackburn. "Talk about the Gillingham game," Dickov says, "but what a bizarre game that one [against Blackburn] was – we should have been 4-0 down at half time.

"I remember a lot about that day," he continues, "I was gutted because I wasn't starting, but after sitting and watching the first half I don't know how Blackburn weren't out of sight at half time.

"But it was the character of the players again. A lot of the players were the same from the year before and we had a fantastic team spirit, we really did. Just before I came on, Ian Bishop came on and slowed the game down. Bish was great because he got us playing the way we wanted to play.

"Then the goals came thick and fast," he says, as City went on to come from 1-0 down to win 4-1, "and I'll never forget all the City fans not even in the stadium, but on the hill at the back."

I then commented on Dickov's ability to score at just the right time. In the game in 1999, he netted with seconds left to keep City's dreams of promotion alive. Then, a year on, he rounded off the win at Ewood Park, to secure a return to the top flight. "I'm a lucky little shit, aren't I?" he says.

It meant the club enjoyed back-to-back promotions, something that Dickov says was never talked about. "We knew we had a decent squad," he says, "Joe brought in the likes of Mark Kennedy that year, who did, no doubt, improve us. But, for me as a player, that was the best group of lads that I played with.

"I wouldn't say back-to-back promotions were expected, but we knew that if we were right we could have done it," he says.

That club that was promoted back to the Premier League was a far cry from the one that Dickov joined in August 1996. He made his debut in a 2-1 defeat against Stoke, coming off the bench at half time. It was a time that would sum up just what turbulence the club was experiencing – the manager that signed him, Alan Ball, resigned after the loss.

"It was turmoil," the striker says, "considering I signed on the Friday and the manager resigned on the Sunday. I'd already had a couple of managers at Arsenal during the preseason and it was ridiculous the number of managers I had from the July-August time to the following January. New managers come in and one likes you or one doesn't, but that seemed to happen every week!

"Joe was a big factor [in turning the club's fortunes around]," he continues, "I think anybody that's played under Joe will tell you that. I think his biggest strength was getting the best out of us as individuals, but then integrating that into a team.

"When Joe and David Bernstein came in, there was an air of stability about the club, which had never been there in the time that I was there. We didn't know where the club was going, whether it was going to be sold, who the manager was going to be... And, even when a manager came in, because of the shambles that it was sometimes, we didn't know how long he was going to stay.

"But Joe came in and steadied the ship," he says. "He gave everyone their confidence back and got us playing again. He made us realise how lucky we were to be footballers and how lucky we were to be at a club like Man City."

The beginning of the end for Dickov's first spell with the Blues came just after the 2000-01 season. City had narrowly missed out on Premier League survival, as losing to Ipswich at Portman Road in the penultimate game of the campaign confirmed the club's relegation. Not long after the final game of the year – a 2-1 defeat at home to Chelsea – the board sacked Joe Royle.

"Kevin [Keegan] for some reason didn't think I was tall enough or aggressive enough to play in Division One. Tall enough, maybe. But aggressive enough? I don't think he could have been further from the truth."

"Everybody – the lads to a man – was disappointed," he says. "Joe was great. He wasn't just your manager, he was your friend as well. You could go and speak to him about anything. As players, and especially being at City at that time, you get used to managers coming and going.

"You have managers that you do get on better with and are your favourites," he continues, "but I don't remember any member of that squad moaning or grumbling when Joe was in charge. We were all gutted when he left because we all knew he could have got the best out of us."

Dickov moved on under Royle's replacement, Kevin Keegan. "I was disappointed," he says, "because Kevin for some reason didn't think I was tall enough or aggressive enough to play in Division One. Tall enough, maybe. But aggressive enough? I don't think he could have been further from the truth.

"I went to see Kevin before the game with Notts County on 11th September," Dickov says, "he kept telling me I'd get my chance and to bide my time. He named the team against Notts County, which was a team of fringe players, and I still wasn't there.

"So I went to see him and said, 'What's happening? Everyone's getting a chance, but you don't seem to be giving me a chance, is it personal?' As a person, I'm somebody that, if someone isn't happy with what I'm doing then I'll do everything I can to try and make it right. I was working hard in training. I felt fit and I felt sharp.

"And Kevin just kept saying to me, 'You'll get your chance, you'll get your chance.' He wouldn't say anything else and that chance never came, so it was something I was disappointed with him about. I let him know that.

"The Notts County game," he continues, "I came on in as a sub and scored. Then the following Saturday I wasn't even in the 20-man squad. Throughout that year, he then told me that if a club came in for me that he'd let me go and I found out that various clubs came in for me, but he didn't let me go.

"Then, when I eventually signed for Leicester, he didn't want me to go there. He wanted me to go to a [Third Division] side. I was told by other people at the time that he didn't want me to go there because he knew I'd do well."

However, the move to Leicester wasn't the end of Dickov's City career – he was to return, but ended up playing against them on a number of occasions first. He scored at Eastlands in a 3-0 Foxes win, before he did the same for Blackburn in a 1-1 draw – having moved to Ewood Park in 2004.

In the mean time, a lot had changed at City once more. Kevin Keegan departed in March 2005 and was replaced on a caretaker basis by Stuart Pearce. Having ended the season well, 'Psycho' was given the job permanently and had a good start to the 2005-06 campaign. But a poor finish meant that the club slid down the table and, in order to strengthen for the 2006-07 season, Pearce made some necessary additions to his squad.

One of them was a returning Paul Dickov.

"Even with the problems I had under Kevin," Dickov says, "I still didn't want to leave the football club. I loved it there and had a massive affinity with the fans, the club, the people who worked there and everything to do with it.

"I spoke to Stuart quite a few times," he continues, "he knew I was out of contract at Blackburn. Blackburn had offered me a new deal, but once I knew I had the chance to go back to City there was no way I was turning down that. People say you should never go back, and looking back perhaps that was right.

"I never regretted the decision to go back," he says. "I would have regretted it more if I hadn't. I'd be sitting here now wondering why I didn't go back.

"I was a bit unfortunate. I knew Stuart brought be back as much for what I could do off the pitch as what I could do on it. The squad were quite a quiet bunch and there were a few kids there. From playing against Stuart and with him for a short time at City, he knew exactly what I was like.

"Something as you get older, you naturally start to talk to the younger ones – and we had a lot of young kids," he continues, "Micah Richards, Stevie Ireland, Nedum [Onuoha], Michael Johnson... and I used to try and help them as much as I could.

"But I didn't help myself that season," he says, when I ask about his injuries, "I broke my foot early on and I played for nine or ten weeks with my foot broken because I didn't want to miss any games. If I'd have had that sorted straight away, I might have got more games. I also struggled with my back, which, at the time, I didn't realise the extent of the injury.

"In hindsight, injury-wise I probably shouldn't have played a lot of the games I did. But I only did it because I loved being where I was and I loved playing football."

"...it's humbling for me because I don't think it's any secret that I'm a City fan... People might say Aguero's stolen my thunder, but there was nobody more delighted than me when he scored that goal."

That season turned out to be Dickov's last at City and in the Premier League. After loan spells with Crystal Palace and Blackpool, he moved back to Leicester before joining Leeds and Oldham, finishing at the latter as player-manager. He went on to become the Latics' gaffer for roughly two and a half seasons, until he resigned in January 2013. For the start of the 2013-14 season, the ex-striker was appointed manager of Doncaster Rovers and it's in their press room where we met to do the interview.

"I'm loving management," he says, "it's a learning experience for me and the time I had at Oldham was fantastic to give me a grounding. I'm at a club in Doncaster now that is a stable club and the opportunity for me to manage in the Championship at my age is fantastic for me.

"The day-to-day stuff is brilliant for me," he continues, "I'm out on the football pitch and we've got a good group that all get on well."

I couldn't leave without asking his reaction to another famous City goal, which came just in the nick of time. The words 'last-minute' and 'Manchester City' used to be synonymous with Paul Dickov, but now the name Sergio Aguero more than likely tops the list in fans' memories, after the effort against QPR in May 2012 that secured the Premier League title for the club.

"It's fantastic [for the two goals to be compared]," he says, "and it's humbling for me because I don't think it's any secret that I'm a City fan myself. So to have that sort of comparison thrown at me, I get quite embarrassed sometimes – especially when you look at the quality of Aguero to the quality that I had. It's chalk and cheese!

"People might say Aguero's stolen my thunder, but there was nobody more delighted than me when he scored that goal."

10 SHAUN GOATER

It quite often goes unnoticed how much hard work Shaun Goater had to put in at Manchester City to become a club legend. The man who would score goal after goal to the background noise of the fans roaring, 'Feed the Goat and he will score' didn't always have it as easy as that in a blue shirt. The turnaround was, frankly, remarkable – as the Bermudian was regularly faced with questions about his ability to put the ball in the net, while week after week he answered them, eventually finishing as the club's top scorer in four successive seasons.

Goater signed for City on deadline day of the 1997-98 campaign, shortly after Joe Royle had taken charge of the club. He was moving from Bristol City – a team that, at the time, was sitting second in Division Two and would end up going on to win promotion – to the Blues, who would end up dropping out of Division One at the end of the year.

> ## CITY CAREER STATS
>
> **Apps:** 212 (23 sub)
> **Goals:** 103
>
> **Signed:** March 1998
> **Left:** June 2003
>
> **Debut:** Bradford (a), 1998
> **Result:** 2-1 defeat

"I was definitely excited," the Bermudian striker says about hearing the Blues were chasing his signature, "it was a club that I felt could either make or break a player's career. I was one who was certainly on the up in the lower leagues and I felt this was the stature of club that I needed to be at to be able to test myself at the highest level – and it eventually proved to be right, as well."

Goater joined the Blues with seven matches of the campaign remaining and with the club scrapping for survival in Division One. He scored three times in the final games of the season, but it wasn't enough to save the club from a relegation that had looked inevitable for some time. When he first put his name down on the dotted line, was he aware of just exactly what he was letting himself in for?

"I think it dawned on me about two or three weeks in," he says. "I was coming from Bristol City, who were flying, and the confidence was high and we were scoring goals. I had come to a team where confidence wasn't so high – in fact, where we used to train at Platt Lane, fans used to come in their cars at lunchtimes and basically stand outside the fence and say, 'You're rubbish!'

"That was very draining and it drained confidence and team morale very quickly," he continues. "That was a unique experience."

Goater himself had to win the City fans over. When he arrived at the Blues, for whatever reason, he wasn't seen as a good signing and the Maine Road crowd just didn't take to him or his style of play. "It's funny," he says, "because at all the clubs I'd been at, I'd always been the top goalscorer. And even though the fans didn't take to me for the first year or year and a half, I was still the top goalscorer, so I couldn't really figure out why.

> **"I had come to a team where confidence wasn't so high – in fact, where we used to train at Platt Lane, fans used to come in their cars at lunchtimes and basically stand outside the fence and say, 'You're rubbish!'"**

"All I did at that time was think, 'Okay – who do they love?' and they loved Paul Dickov. So every time we had training sessions when the coach would say, 'Get a ball between two', I would strategically try to get with Paul to really observe his ways and see what he was like.

"So I just took from his game," he continues, "I thought the fans loved what he did, so I tried to put that in my game – along with continuing to score the goals. Paul had an unbelievable work rate. He had a real tenacity about him – as a striker, he had an attitude much like a defender. So I tried to put that into my game and that, eventually, helped me to win the fans over."

From when the striker joined City, the Blues were always changing division at the end of the season – up or down – right up until his final campaign. Whilst at Maine Road, Goater went through two relegations and three promotions, but says he didn't find it that difficult to wipe the slate clean and start again each year.

"As a player," he says, "you don't really get too caught up in the off the field stuff, you just really focus on your game. You know when you're doing a good job and you know when you're not. So, for me, it was easy because, from my point of view, the first year challenge was to prove myself – not so much for me, but for the fans, because the first year I was top goalscorer and they didn't like me. So the challenge I had was to continue being a top goalscorer, but win them over too.

"So I had that focus," he continues. "It allowed me to go into every game not taking anything for granted. There were some players who, going into a game, knew they could make two or three mistakes and not really get any flak for it. Whereas, I couldn't go into a game and make one mistake, because I knew I would get the flak – sometimes whether it was my fault or not!

"That kept me on edge. It kept me very motivated to prove Joe Royle right for having the confidence to sign me and then prove to myself that I could belong there and play at that level and higher. Then, eventually, the fans started to see what I had to contribute."

Soon enough, the fans were on his side and Goater had his own bespoke chant from the Maine Road faithful. Sung to the tune of *Bread of Heaven*, the City crowd began to belt out, 'Feed the Goat and he will score'. How did Goater feel when he first heard it, having worked so hard to earn the fans' support?

"Once hearing the song, I knew it was mine," he says, "and it made the hairs stand up on the back of my neck. That was the first sign in my head that I'd won the fans over, but because of the journey I'd had in the first year, I was never going to allow that love that they had in singing the song to make me think, 'Oh, I've made it now.'

"For me, I was going into every game still with the determination to prove I could be a good player for the club. So I had the same sort of psyche as when the fans didn't like me. I didn't get too caught up in that, 'They're singing songs about you now, you can relax.' I didn't at all."

In the build-up to the Play-Off Final in 1999, City eased past Wigan in the second of the two semi-finals. The only goal of the game was scored by City's Bermudian striker, but the TV replays proved inconclusive at the time as to whether the effort should have stood – with commentator Alistair Mann believing the referee had originally ruled it out. As the cross came over, Goater appeared to chest the ball towards the net. Latics' goalkeeper Roy Carroll couldn't keep it out, but many of the Wigan defenders were appealing for handball.

From the camera angle, it was very difficult to tell whether the ball had struck the Bermudian's arm after it had hit his chest. There's only one man who can clear it all up.

"No, it wasn't handball," Goater says, "and there's no need for me to sit here today and lie about it. No, the ball has come across and I've dipped my shoulder and it's hit me on my chest.

"It's funny because the referee for that game works in Bermuda now," he continues. "I was with some friends and he actually bumped into me. And he asked me, 'So, tell me Shaun, was that a handball?' and I said, 'Of course it wasn't!' And I was laughing because it was funny he was asking me all these years later.

"He actually asked me immediately after, as well. So he must have had some doubt to think maybe it was," he says, "but I can categorically say it was off my chest and I've chested it in."

The result allowed City to have the chance of a game at Wembley, with the main prize being promotion back to Division One at the first attempt.

"I had some nerves," Goater tells me, "but I learned to control the nerves because it's my body telling me that I'm excited about the occasion. But you need to be in control because you can waste a lot of energy on big games like that by being so excited and having the adrenalin within you.

"I actually woke up earlier than I normally do and I looked at the clock and thought I could lie in for another half hour or so," he continues, "but then my mind remembered, 'It's today' and I couldn't go back to sleep. It was exciting to get up and prepare for the game slowly, because Wembley's certainly not a place you want to go and lose."

However, it certainly looked like City could end up being on the losing side. Two goals down and with the 90 minute mark approaching, Goater tells me he was feeling dejected: "I was thinking, 'This has all been a waste and we've got it all to do next year.'

"...the referee for that game works in Bermuda now. I was with some friends and he actually bumped into me. And he asked me, 'So, tell me Shaun, was that a handball?' and I said, 'Of course it wasn't!'"

"That thought went through my mind when they scored their second goal," he says. "Their player Carl Asaba went off and he was high-fiving the players and all that. In a way, that wound me up, but at the same time I was thinking, 'We can't lose this game.' And at that point, Kevin Horlock was saying, 'Come on!' as in 'Don't give up' or 'Let's go to the end'. I look around and I feel the same – and then when he scored and we get the ball to go back for kick-off, I was starting to think, 'Is it just a consolation? Yeah, maybe...'

"But then Kevin Horlock gave me the ball and I've had a touch and gone to shoot. Their lad has put a great tackle on me and the ball's deflected to Paul [Dickov] and that's when he scored. And, at that point, I loved him more than anything!

"I was tackled in the build-up to both the goals," he jokes. "Paul knows – I told him – that I was passing it to him!"

The game could have been so different midway through the second half. A ball in from the left flank missed everybody and fell to Goater at the back post. He opted not to pull it back for Dickov who was waiting in the middle and instead tried to place it inside Bartram's near post. He beat the goalkeeper, but not the frame of the goal, the side-footed shot ricocheting behind off the base of the post.

> "I think Nicky [Weaver] thought, 'Sod that, I'd better save a couple!' I think somebody must have said to him, 'Shaun's the fifth penalty taker, so we need you to save at least two...'"

It's hardly surprising, though, given how the game ended and the dramatic nature of the final few minutes, that Goater has no recollection of it happening: "I hit the post?" he asks, when I put the question to him. "After the game, we obviously celebrated, but you don't look back at the game in total depth – that game was done and dusted. I suppose if we'd lost, I'd have dissected it and gone, 'That's how close we were and had that chance gone in, it'd be a different game.'

"But I actually don't remember hitting the post at 0-0."

However, had City won the game in normal time, the match probably wouldn't be as fondly remembered as it is now. Through the comeback in 90 minutes and a non-event of extra time, City were forced to face a penalty shootout. With the score at 3-1 to the Blues, Guy Butters missed Gillingham's fourth spot-kick, meaning it was game over – and the fans didn't get to see who would have made the long walk to take the final kick.

"It was me," Goater says, before laughing and adding, "and I think Nicky [Weaver] thought, 'Sod that, I'd better save a couple!' I think somebody must have said to him, 'Shaun's the fifth penalty taker, so we need you to save at least two and hope they miss another one!'

"Penalties, for me, is about who wants it on the day," he says, more seriously, "you look around and the manager says, 'I need brave players to take a penalty,' and you can tell those who don't want to because they're right there next to the gaffer, then straight away they look away almost as if to say, 'I know you're not talking to me!' I wasn't scared to take one, so therefore I said I would.

"He [Joe Royle] then sorted out the order and I was last. I was pleased because I think I was going to go for a little dink down the middle," he says, before chuckling at the idea. "It's easy to say that now – I'd have actually leathered it!"

Goater is a man who is very driven. Throughout his career, he's proved people wrong on the pitch – as City won promotion from Division Two, there were questions about whether the Bermudian could score goals in the league above, but he swiftly provided the answers by once more finishing as the club's top scorer. Those same questions were put to him again following promotion to the Premier League and Goater answered them in exactly the same way.

"That's probably one of the biggest motivating things about me," he says, "I'm one of those that really wants to prove people wrong. When they say I can't do this or can't achieve that, for some innate reason there's something in me that comes out and says, 'I can do this!' and I get a focus and a determination. It's like I want to prove to myself that I can do it and that becomes my goal.

"I have a strong belief that proving people wrong motivates me no end, and I've realised that as time's gone on. I wouldn't have thought that in my mid-20s.

"It almost sounds arrogant, but I think almost everything I've really put my mind to I've achieved – from wanting to be a professional player, to wanting to play in the Premier League, to even after football and wanting to set up a semi-professional team in Bermuda."

Following City's second promotion, this one back to the Premier League, Goater might have felt like his chances of remaining the club's top scorer were going to be limited. In came George Weah and Paulo Wanchope, adding to his competition for places. Then, in December, Darren Huckerby joined the Blues. And, on top of all of that, the Bermudian was injured for the start of the campaign.

Despite those setbacks, Goater was upbeat: "I was excited," he says, "we'd been promoted to the Premier League and there were these top quality players that were coming, too. I was looking at them in training and thinking, 'This is the quality I want to be around – this is the quality I want to absorb from and learn from and play with.'

"So I always loved that competition because I wanted to play with that kind of quality. I didn't look at it like they were coming to take my place, I was thinking, 'I could play with him' and they could see it was something I looked forward to as well."

In the end, Goater was the club's top scorer, but everything wasn't rosy from a striking perspective. Weah left in the October after just two-and-a-half months at Maine Road, while Wanchope had a falling out with the manager and missed a huge chunk of games. With the club struggling for goals, there was a lot of pressure on Goater to keep up his previous scoring rate – but the trouble for the Bermudian was that, in the top flight, City just weren't creating chances.

His 11 goals that year saw him top the club's charts, but it wasn't enough to save the Blues from relegation. At the end of that season, City also changed managers – something that possibly began the process of Goater's decision to leave the club. He tells me he couldn't believe it when he heard the news of Joe Royle's sacking.

"It was a big surprise," he says, "I was out and about with my wife and just heard on the radio that Joe Royle had left by mutual agreement. And I thought, 'Hold on – two days ago we were in work and now he's gone?'

"So I started calling one or two of the other players up to see if they knew anything," he continues, "I was feeling like we were on the rise and I was wondering if it was the right decision. We had been relegated but I was thinking, 'Joe could get us back.' I had belief in him – 100 per cent belief – so it was a real surprise to me.

> **"It was a big surprise. I was out and about with my wife and just heard on the radio... I started calling one or two of the other players up to see if they knew anything... I was feeling like we were on the rise and I was wondering if it was the right decision."**

"He had belief in me and his belief was in his actions in playing me week in, week out," he says, "but no matter how much you like a manager or dislike a manager, you have to dust yourself off and just get on with it."

Under Kevin Keegan, Goater's time at City wasn't easy. He did, however, have one of the best goalscoring seasons in his career in the year the Blues won Division One to bounce back to the Premier League, netting 32 times in 46 appearances in all competitions.

"It was a joy because, as a forward player, he [Keegan] wanted the team to create opportunities and score goals," Goater says, "it was because of players like Ali Benarbia and Eyal Berkovic, who created so many opportunities. All I was doing was making sure that my finishing was spot on because I knew I'd get opportunities."

But, after being a figurehead of the City attack in a team playing free-flowing and attacking football, the Bermudian found his chances limited when back in the top flight. Nicolas Anelka signed and, once again, Goater was injured for the beginning of the 2002-03 campaign.

In what turned out to be his final season at Maine Road, the Bermudian found himself starting most games from the bench. He was later critical of Kevin Keegan's management style in his book, who he says he thought would rather pick the players he signed for the club over himself.

"Joe Royle and Kevin Keegan were almost like opposites," he tells me, "it was a shift because we were a working class team. It was about everyone working hard for one another: there were no big time Charlies... we all had average cars and it was only when Kevin Keegan came that the lifestyle changed for the players. You started to see one or two Mercedes coming in, then BMWs and Ferraris...

"Keegan was about playing out from the back and playing through the thirds," he continues. "Sometimes if we'd been outplayed what I wondered was, 'Where are the tactics for us to outplay them? We're halfway through the game, what shift or adjustments are we making?' And his philosophy was, 'You are good enough to go out there and outplay them'.

"It was a learning curve for me and that's what I found to be the difference [between the two managers]," he says.

However, Goater did hit a landmark in his final year with the club. Following his 71st minute winner at The Hawthorns, the Bermudian was handed a start in the final Manchester Derby at Maine Road. The Blues hadn't won against United in over a decade – with the sides meeting 16 times since their last victory.

City rose to the occasion, however. Nicolas Anelka opened the scoring four minutes into the game (netting when Fabien Barthez parried Goater's initial effort), before Ole Gunnar Solskjaer equalised a short time later. But it was then that City's Bermudian striker started to leave his mark on the match.

Midway through the first half, Marc-Vivien Foe played a long ball over the top, but sliced it horribly. With the ball looking like it would make it to the byline, United fullback Gary Neville tried to let it roll out for a goal kick – but Goater chased him down. The striker stole possession and bore down on Barthez's goal from a tight angle, before smashing the shot into the bottom corner, giving the Blues the lead for the second time of the afternoon.

Very little had been made of it pre-match, but that first half strike put the Bermudian's total number of goals for the Blues to 99 and one

> "I dinked one [goal] over Barthez – who was a World Cup winning goalkeeper... The goal the City fans love that I've equally come to love as much is the one that [Gary] Neville fed me! And it was a great ball by him as well!"

away from triple figures. He didn't have to wait long to make it a century – six minutes into the second half he took his chance.

Foe won a loose ball in midfield and knocked it wide to Niclas Jensen. The left back swung it inside towards Berkovic who, with a brilliant one-touch layoff, dropped the ball into the path of Goater, who was holding off Laurent Blanc. As Barthez closed him down, the City striker dinked it over the top of the goalkeeper and into the net.

They were not only special goals in terms of Goater's personal tally at City, but also because Manchester United was the club that had originally brought the Bermudian to England. The Reds had the striker on trial in 1989, where he earned a professional contract, but didn't break into the first team at Old Trafford.

"My 99th and 100th goals against United showed what I had achieved and what I wanted to achieve," he says, "I wanted to show that I was capable of playing at that level, making a mark and playing well. I did get Man of the Match in that game, but that was really about proving to myself.

"The goals," he continues, "I think were good goals. I dinked one over Barthez – who was a World Cup winning goalkeeper, so I took a lot of joy in that. The goal the City fans love that I've equally come to love as much is the one that Neville fed me!

"And it was a great ball by him as well!"

Until recently, Goater's final ever goal for the club was a Premier League record breaker (since beaten by Nicklas Bendtner for Arsenal against Tottenham). With the Blues losing the return derby at Old Trafford, Keegan introduced both the Bermudian and Ali Benarbia from the bench with a little over four minutes to play. The midfielder touched a free kick back to Shaun Wright-Phillips, who crossed into the box – where Goater had escaped his marker and nodded it into the net, a mere nine seconds after joining the action.

"I was motivated," he says, "it was my last year and I certainly wasn't starting regularly and I knew my part in the game was coming on [from the bench] and that Keegan had belief in other players to start. I knew my part was coming on for 20 minutes... 15 minutes... ten minutes...

"It's funny because I was coming on and scoring," he continues, "but my time was getting less. If you look at the records of the last ten games I played, I was coming on with about 30 minutes to go and I'd score. Then the next game, I'd come on and it'd be 25 minutes and I'd score. And it got down to a point where it was about seven minutes and I'd score and Kevin Keegan must have been thinking, 'This bloody boy just keeps scoring; I'm giving him less and less time and he keeps bloody scoring.'

"I was motivated to say, 'Okay, maybe I'm not your first choice, but I'm still going to give you that headache by scoring,' and maybe he would consider starting me," he says, "so that's all I did. I just tried to perform the best I could.

"Kevin Horlock realised," he continues, "he used to say, 'You're not getting on until there's only a few minutes left. Robbie Fowler is either going to score or miss ten chances, but you won't get on until there's about ten minutes left.' And we had this little joke that whenever Robbie Fowler missed a chance in the second half, I would get up and warm up.

"Then the fans used to give this roar of, 'Feed the Goat' and a couple of times I'd done it when he [Keegan] was stood there analysing the game," he says. "I'd get up and I'd nudge Kevin [Horlock] or he'd nudge me and I'd say 'Watch this.'

"I'd then sprint down the touchline," Goater continues, "and when a player sprints down the touchline, it looks like he's been told to warm up. So the fans would think I was coming on and start singing even louder. I'd do another sprint down to the bench and I'm doing my movements and my stretches and I would look out of the corner of my eye and see the gaffer. He'd look out the corner of his eye and see what I was doing and then there was pressure and he must have been thinking, 'I've got to put him on!'

"That was only for the last ten games or so and it got me on for some minutes."

Shortly before the end of the season, Goater announced that he would be leaving the club in the summer. Having fallen down the pecking order and entering the final stages of his career, he wanted to be playing regularly – something that wasn't guaranteed at City.

The final match of the campaign was also the last game that would ever be staged at City's Maine Road stadium. Typically, the Blues lost 1-0 to Southampton. However, captain for the day, was Shaun Goater and he was given a rapturous round of applause by the fans as he left the game on 63 minutes, with the introduction of Robbie Fowler.

"It was awesome," he says, "I was also captain for a period with Joe Royle, but that was one of my proudest moments playing for the club. In the first year and a half, I took some serious stick from the fans. But it was my goals and my endeavour that turned that around, so when I achieved being the captain it was a really proud moment. It showed I had come on leaps and bounds and I had put the hard work in.

> "In the first year and a half, I took some serious stick from the fans. But it was my goals and my endeavor that turned that around, so when I achieved being the captain it was a really proud moment."

"So the last game of the season was emotional," he continues. "It was all about trying to contain the emotions and I'm seeing banners saying things like, 'Feed the Goat' and I'm thinking, 'This is the last game at Maine Road and this club has been here 80 years and people are finding the need to put up banners of Shaun Goater on this historical day, in parallel to it being the final game there for the club.'

"And that's what hit me that was the fans showing their love and their appreciation of me," he says, "so that was emotional to see that. I remember warming up with Robbie Fowler and he was saying, 'These people love you here.' And it was a bizarre conversation because, at that time, I realised that this was coming from Robbie Fowler – someone I looked up to playing and goalscoring. And he was saying to me that he wanted the fans to love him as much as they loved me!

"It was hard to contain the emotions and it did affect my performance," he says.

Even after leaving City, though, Goater's relationship with the Blues' fans didn't end. By a quirk of the fixture list, the Bermudian's final ever game in English football before he retired came for Southend against Bristol City – the club that Joe Royle signed him from in 1998.

In the crowd for that game were roughly 400 Manchester City fans.

"We had three sets of supporters showing appreciation of my time at their clubs," he says, "so it was special. They made a whole Bermuda Day of it, with Bermuda Gombeys [traditional dance groups], dancers and drums – all sorts of stuff like that. It was emotional and going off, I broke down in tears because I loved the game.

"It was very special because it was three sets of fans all congratulating me on my career and giving their appreciation of me being at their club."

I interviewed Shaun twice for this book. The first was at the North West Football Awards in 2013, where he was to give out the Manager of the Year award – he had been due to present Sir Alex Ferguson with the prize, had the former Manchester United boss been available to go to the event. Instead, he handed it to his number two.

The second interview, however, was at a local football club where he was doing some coaching work towards his UEFA Licenses. He explains to me that he just couldn't stay away from the English game – having originally gone back home and set up the Bermuda Hogges, a football team based in the country's capital, Hamilton.

"I went back home," he says about the end of his playing career, "and was just looking to get some sunshine one me. After being there for seven years, I decided I had had enough sunshine and missed the cold and rainy weather, so I came back to Manchester to pursue coaching and management."

11 TERRY COOKE

When I had already begun the interviews for this book and knew that I was going to fight tooth and nail to speak to every single one of the 1999 Play-Off Final team, the issue of contacting some of the players who were difficult to track down came into my head. As time's gone on, the team has slowly lost touch with each other – as they've all moved clubs or retired from the game. One of those I was particularly worried about contacting was Terry Cooke, a Solihull-born right-winger City signed from Manchester United.

In the end, I needn't have had too many worries, but it wasn't my initial reaction. I put his name into Google and found that, after leaving the Blues for Grimsby, his career took him around the world. He went on to play for Sheffield Wednesday, before joining Colorado Rapids in the MLS. After four years there, he moved to Australia, signing for North Queensland Fury, before finishing his career with Gabala in Azerbaijan.

It was at this point I was beginning to wonder if it would be possible to speak to him at all, but a mere three minutes later, I'd found that he was now working for a sports marketing company in the United States and now lived back in Colorado. On top of that, his office contact details were on the website. So I worked out the time difference, called him at a reasonable hour and arranged an interview. Sadly, he wasn't planning a return trip to the UK, so we had to speak over the phone.

The very next day, I call him up once more and ask if he had enough time to chat and is ready to go. "Just let me put the dog out," he says, his voice still carrying a heavy Midlands twang despite years of living in various cities around the world.

Cooke's move to City came midway through the 1998-99 season. It was originally a loan from United, following his previous loan spell to another club in the Blues' division. In fact, Cooke played in one of the matches that began the turnaround for the club's form – a Boxing Day trip to the Racecourse Ground – but he

CITY CAREER STATS

Apps: 41 (8 sub)
Goals: 8

Signed: January 1999
Left: July 2002

Debut: Fulham (h), 1999
Result: 3-0 victory

played for the home side that day, Wrexham.

"Back in 1997, I'd done my cruciate," Cooke says. "To get me back playing quicker and sharper, I went to Wrexham on loan after I'd come back from rehab on my knee injury. I had a really good game against Man City and obviously they'd made enquiries about me because my loan period was coming to an end. That's when they came in for me.

"I had been told there was a good chance I'd probably never play again," he says about his injury, "so, for me, I was interested in getting out on loan and getting back fully recovered. I was a young lad and I wanted to play. Luckily, City came in for me and it meant I didn't have to travel as much – every day I'd been travelling back and forth to Wrexham."

"I had been told there was a good chance I'd probably never play again, so, for me, I was interested in getting out on loan and getting back fully recovered."

Cooke joined the Blues in January 1999. After impressive displays in his first two months with the club, Joe Royle decided to sign him on a permanent basis, securing his services for a reported £1m. City were unbeaten in Cooke's first nine games with the club – a spell including five wins and 17 goals – and were beginning to rise from mid-table obscurity.

"They had a good, strong squad," he says of the team he joined, "they'd just been relegated to Division Two and, for me, the timing was good. I think they'd had a culture shock – everyone knows when you drop out of the Premier League it's very hard to get back out of the lower leagues.

"They had a great team, but were struggling and I just came in at the right time and was able to help them transform the fortunes of the club," he continues. "We went on a very good run and just missed out on automatic promotion."

Narrowly missing the automatic promotion places at the end of the season could have had a negative effect on the team, but Cooke tells me that actually the opposite was true: "The lads were buzzing and there was confidence," he says, "We were confident anyway because we'd just been on a long unbeaten run and to end up in the play-offs from where we were was just a bonus.

"Obviously it was disappointing [to miss out on second place]," he continues, "but that didn't bother us. We were at a big club in City who would get over crowds of over 30-thousand at Maine Road every week.

We knew that the momentum was with us and the confidence in the squad was sky high at the time."

Having finished in third place, the Blues played sixth-placed Wigan in the semi-finals. "It was at their old stadium," Cooke says, "and we gave up an early goal. We were the better team over the two legs.

"It was every player's dream to play at a stadium of that magnitude in an important game – whether it's an FA Cup final, a European Cup final... This was just as big in our books, to get the team back up into the higher divisions where it belongs."

Wigan didn't really have many expectations; they were the underdogs and we were the favourites. All the pressure was on our shoulders and to give up an early goal away was crucial. That set the tempo then for the two legs.

"We managed to get an equaliser," he continues, "but then the atmosphere in the second leg at home was unbelievable. It was amazing and to get the club to go to Wembley the way we did was fantastic."

Cooke was only 22 when he was named in City's starting line-up for the Play-Off Final with Gillingham. Despite being a young lad, though, he tells me that the pressure and the occasion didn't get the better of him: "It was a dream come true," he says, "it's that whole cliché.

"It was a dream to play at Wembley – especially the old one before it was demolished. It was a good time for Manchester because we came from behind in a similar manner to what United had done to win the European Cup. It was just as special for us – and if we didn't win that game, you don't know where City would be these days.

"It was a massive game for the club because it transformed the whole history overnight," he continues. "Going into the game, we knew the pressure was on us. We knew it was going to be in front of a full house and we were the favourites. Just to walk out before the game for the warm-ups and to get a feel for the pitch, the atmosphere was amazing. It was every player's dream to play at a stadium of that magnitude in an important game – whether it's an FA Cup final, a European Cup final... This was just as big in our books, to get the team back up into the higher divisions where it belongs."

As for the game itself, Cooke admits that his memories have faded over time. It was a difficult game for the winger and he struggled to get into the form he'd showed in the run-up – though there was an argument that that description fitted most of the City side for the first 89 minutes. Cooke, despite his critics, did get several good balls into the area, but the Blues were unable to capitalise.

"It's weird because when you play in this sort of game, it can often fly past really quickly," Cooke says, "you don't really realise that you've been in the game because the emotions can take over you. We were the better team throughout the game and at half time at 0-0 we knew the game was there for the taking.

"We were the ones who were forcing the issue and going on to try and win the game," he continues. "I thought I had a decent game, but I played better throughout the league campaign. I thought my contribution to the game was good and I thought I put some good deliveries into the box.

"But as the game went on, you could feel the atmosphere in the stadium turning to tension. Obviously, you can pick it up [on the pitch] because the fans know how the game is going and it's getting later and later at 0-0. Anything can happen… which it did!

"Gillingham broke on us twice," he continues, "and I think that was the only time they counter attacked us in the entire game and it led to both goals. To be 2-0 down as late as that – the game was over."

That's certainly how it felt to the fans, too – as Robert Taylor doubled the Gils' lead, thousands of City's supporters headed for the exits, planning for a second season in the third tier. But Kevin Horlock and Paul Dickov had other ideas, and Cooke puts the late drama down to one aspect of the Blues' squad.

"Never to this day have I been in a locker room with a team environment like that one that was at City at that time," he says, "our team spirit and togetherness was fantastic. We all got on well with each other and we had a good bunch of lads who worked hard for each other and that showed to the end. We dug in and never gave up.

"I think we were given a bit of a boost when Tony Pulis took off his forward men," he continues, "obviously, he sat there thinking the job was done and all we needed was one chance [to get back into the game] and that's what we got. We put a few more bodies forward and their keeper came out to the edge of the 18 to make a block, but it ended up at the sweet left foot of Kevin Horlock. It could have ended up in row Z, but he hit it so perfectly it ended up in the net.

"Then, as soon as we saw the board go up for stoppage time, we knew we were back in the game. Then all we needed was one chance and everyone remembers that goal from Paul Dickov, which caused the game to turn on a sixpence. The atmosphere of the stadium changed – it swung in our favour – and we knew we were going to win the game.

"We'd been through too much that season and we could just tell [that City were going to emerge winners] because of the confidence and the attitude of the group," he continues. "We had enough quality on the pitch and we kept plugging away to get our just rewards in the end.

"I still remember the celebrations and seeing all the fans rushing back into the stadium and back into their seats," he continues, "it was just an unbelievable day.

"I still watch it now and again," he continues, "It's a shame that I never got the whole game, but there is stuff on YouTube and now and again I will watch it and reminisce. I'll just have a little watch of it and it still chokes me up a little bit – you look at [Nottingham] Forest or Leeds, if you don't come back up straight away, it can take a long, long time.

"That game, I think, was the turning point for the club. If they hadn't won, they might still be there now."

It was at this point in the interview that the inevitable happened. Just as we were getting to the nitty-gritty of the Play-Off Final, the phone connection dropped and the line went silent. This was soon followed by three bleeps and a repeating, computerised female voice telling me: "Sorry, there is a fault. Please try again."

I disconnected the call at my end and redialled so we could continue.

We pick up the discussion with the game finely poised at 2-1 in second half stoppage time. There was a moment when the ball was knocked out wide to Cooke on the right flank and, with the opportunity to put it into the box, he miss-hit the cross and it dropped over the bar. I ask him if he remembers the moment and what he'd been saying to himself as it went out for a goal kick.

"I'd have been disappointed with the delivery," he says, "part and parcel of my game was my delivery from out wide and it was usually spot on, so I'd have been disappointed in that moment. I know I'd have

> "I still watch it now and again. It's a shame that I never got the whole game, but there is stuff on YouTube and now and again I will watch it and reminisce. I'll just have a little watch of it and it still chokes me up a little bit..."

been really frustrated, especially at that time, and of all the times my final ball wasn't there it was at that moment. I'd always prided myself on that part of my game – my service.

"But I didn't let it affect me and it didn't disrupt me."

And he's right – it didn't. Having battled through extra time and not managed to secure the win, the Blues faced penalties and Cooke's name was down on the list as City's third taker.

"I was up for it," he says. "Joe Royle was asking around the squad who wanted to take a penalty and I put my hand up to say I'd have one. He went round a few of the lads and everybody he asked said they'd take one. I can't remember anybody saying they didn't want one. I had no hesitation and said yes straight away."

Having seen Kevin Horlock score and Paul Dickov miss, there was pressure on Cooke's spot-kick. Gillingham's first two takers had both failed to convert, meaning the winger had the chance to make it 2-0 and give the Blues a solid advantage. He finished nicely into the bottom left corner of the goal, with a right-footed drive – goalkeeper Bartram went the right way, but it was so well placed inside the corner that he couldn't keep it out.

"I knew where I was going to go when I put the ball down and I never looked at the keeper," he explains. "I do remember looking up and seeing the fans behind the goal – they looked about half a mile away! It made the goal look even smaller. It looked like a five-a-side goal to me!

"I always keep my penalties low," he continues, "I picked where I wanted to go, put the ball down and turned away to walk back. As soon as I heard the whistle, I turned and aimed to put it to the keeper's bottom right – my bottom left – and I did. It was a massive relief that it went in.

> **"I do remember looking up and seeing the fans behind the goal – they looked about half a mile away! It made the goal look even smaller. It looked like a five-a-side goal to me!"**

"It was a great penalty," he says, starting to laugh, before adding: "I don't think any keeper could have got it."

However, following on from that game, Cooke fell out of favour with Joe Royle and found himself out of the team not long into the following season. From playing regularly for the club, he found himself soon not even making the bench – with rumours surfacing that the Blues couldn't afford to pay the remaining transfer fee to United if he were to make another appearance.

It was a frustrating time for the winger – whose only first team action came in loans spells at Wigan, Sheffield Wednesday (twice), and Grimsby, with Cooke making just 30 appearances in two seasons at various different clubs. By the time Joe Royle had been replaced by Kevin Keegan, the winger wasn't in the first team plans and was allowed to leave on a free transfer.

He joined Grimsby, before switching back to Sheffield Wednesday. Then, on leaving the Owls, Cooke decided to take on a whole new challenge and left the English game completely, opting to sign for Colorado Rapids in the MLS.

> "While I was at City, ITV Digital collapsed. That money had been bankrolling clubs and it meant there were thousands of players looking for a job at the same time..."

"While I was at City," he says, "ITV Digital collapsed. That money had been bankrolling clubs and it meant there were thousands of players looking for a job at the same time as when I left City. It was a good job I'd been on loan to Grimsby because I think they were the only club willing to take me – and that was because I'd been there.

"I stayed there a year and then faced the same situation," he continues. "I went on to sign for Sheffield Wednesday, but I broke my leg. Their financial situation was quite bad and they ended up releasing a lot of players and I just felt like I needed a change.

"I'd kept in touch with Ian Bishop from City and he put me in touch with his agent in America and the rest is history," he says. "I've been here ever since: it was the luck of the draw with the way the system works here [in the USA]. The agent contacted clubs, and Colorado Rapids said they'd have a look at me – so I came over for a couple of weeks. And that was it – I ended up signing for Colorado.

"I ended up having a very good four-and-a-half years here in the MLS. Denver's an absolutely beautiful place, and I was able to re-invent myself and make a name for myself because nobody knew who I was. And it was probably one of the best decisions I've ever made.

"It's a fantastic country and the game's grown over here. It's getting bigger and better, and it's really taking off now – people don't realise what a good, strong league the MLS is. So I was lucky to join when I did and I was very fortunate to be given the chance to come over."

While playing for Colorado Rapids, Cooke came up against a former Manchester United teammate – in a game that went below the radar for a lot of the British press. David Beckham, plying his trade at LA Galaxy, was on the losing side when the two ex-Reds faced off, with the Rapids winning to the tune of four goals to nil.

"It was the first game of the season," he says, "and we played at altitude. We were a very strong team at home because of that. They came in from sea level and we hit the ground running from that day. It was a full house and it was nice because I got to see Becks and I'd not seen him for years, not since we both lived in Manchester.

"It was nice to see an old friend," he continues, "and it was nice I was on the winning team."

Despite now residing in the USA, Cooke didn't end his career in the MLS: "My contract came up at Colorado," he says, "and I like to travel and had a taste for it. I think travelling makes me a better person and I got to see other environments and play in other countries. When you're in England, you get stuck in a certain mentality.

"The chance came up to play in the A-League [in Australia] for half a season," he continues, "these opportunities don't come around that often, so I ended up taking it with both hands. And then I ended up playing [at North Queensland Fury] with Robbie Fowler as well – who had also played for City.

> "The chance came up to play in the A-League for half a season. These opportunities don't come around too often, so I ended up taking it with both hands. And then I ended up playing with Robbie Fowler as well – who had also played for City."

"To be able to play with people like him and with people from all over the world just helps to make me more open minded," he says, "and because I wanted to go into coaching after I finished, the opportunity came up to move to Azerbaijan."

Cooke's final club was Gabala, competing in the Azerbaijan Premier League. "Tony Adams was the manager," he says, "and for me to go and be able to work with someone I'd seen play at Old Trafford when I was at United, someone who'd captained Arsenal and was an England international, was another opportunity I couldn't turn down."

Since retiring from playing, Cooke has returned to the USA, where he now works for a sports marketing company as one of their international representatives. It's a completely different step for someone who was interested in coaching, so how did he end up making such a move?

"I'd always been interested in the business side of the game," he says. "I do miss being on the field and I would like to go into coaching. I was actually offered an assistant coach role with one MLS side last year [2012-13], but I wasn't in a position to go and do it and I didn't want to leave Denver at the time.

"Being in the MLS, you're travelling every other weekend," he continues, "it's not like in England where you jump on a team bus and you're back home the next night. In America, you leave and it takes a whole weekend because you've got to get on board a plane to go to a different state. So, when I was playing, it was hard for my family that I was leaving every other weekend – and then I went to Australia and Azerbaijan and came back each time, too.

"The job came around too quickly and that's why I turned it down. I just wanted to be in a position where I was settled for a bit. Right now, I just want to relax. Coaching is something I'd like to do and being in the business side of the game means it keeps me up to date and I'm still in the game in some capacity."

12 GARETH TAYLOR

When Gareth Taylor joined the action in the 1999 Division Two Play-Off Final, he probably didn't realise what he was letting himself in for. There were five minutes left on the clock and the Blues had just fallen a goal behind when Joe Royle sacrificed a defender in Lee Crooks to go all out attack. In an all-or-nothing game, there's no point in holding back when losing so late on.

Two minutes after Royle switched to a 3-4-3 setup, with Taylor joining Dickov and Goater up top, Gillingham scored again and it looked like it was game over. The second goal for the Gills was scored by Gareth Taylor's namesake Robert – who would go on to sign for the Blues the following season – and that strike caused confusion to one of my friends on a school trip that day.

There should probably be some backstory. I – and some of my friends – were on a primary school camping holiday in Anglesey on the day of the 1999 Play-Off Final. Having got a ticket for Wembley, my dad drove the 110 miles from Manchester to

CITY CAREER STATS

Apps: 53 (19 sub)
Goals: 10

Signed: November 1998
Left: July 2001

Debut: Luton (a), 1998
Result: 1-1 draw

Anglesey to pick me up. From there, we did the 280-mile journey to the national stadium, before heading home for the night in Manchester – another 199 miles. He then finished that up by dropping me off at the campsite, meaning a 220-mile round trip, the next morning. As an 11-year-old boy, I thought nothing of it, but now as a 26-year-old adult and a driver, I dread to think how much damage was done to his wallet with just the petrol costs for an 809 mile journey in a Peugeot 405, carrying four people. Let alone everything else, like food and hotels.

It's here where my friend Will comes into the equation. He normally sat with us at home games at Maine Road, but for reasons I can't remember chose not to have his ticket to Wembley and remained at Anglesey despite the offer to come with us. Listening on the radio in Wales and knowing the score was 1-0, he began celebrating when the commentator announced that Taylor had scored – only to later realise that it was the wrong one. I've since been told by our class teacher that he threw his replica City shirt in a Welsh bin out of frustration and had to go and fish it out later.

Incidentally, having Manchester United fans sharing our tent too, when I was crying inside Wembley at 2-0 and at 2-1, I was ready to go back to Anglesey solely to pick up the rest of my belongings and continue home, rather than complete the holiday.

However, this isn't an account of what happened to me and my mates that day – so back to the City centre forward. Coming on with only a few minutes to play and with the pressure on to change the game, what did the manager say to him, given how bad things looked like they were going?

"I think he said something like, 'All the best, son, go and enjoy yourself!' and I nearly looked at him and started laughing," he says, "especially as they went on to score that second goal. I think he [Joe Royle] was resigned to the fact that that was it.

"This was my third Wembley Play-Off Final and I'd already lost the first two," he continues, "I lost with Bristol Rovers and I lost with Sheffield United. Then this was another one where I was thinking, 'I'm going to lose another one here, now, this is three on the bounce...'

> "This was my third Wembley Play-Off Final and I'd already lost the first two... Then this was another one where I was thinking, 'I'm going to lose another one here, now, this is three on the bounce...'"

"You never know," he says, about whether he felt things could change from 2-0. "People probably weren't feeling that confident even when Kevin [Horlock] scored."

One of the centre forward's most important contributions to the 1998-99 season came in a home game in between Christmas and New Year. City, playing Stoke, had gone in at half time trailing and were looking like they were going to slump to another defeat – what would have been their seventh of the campaign. But an equaliser from Paul Dickov put the Blues on the front foot and, with just five minutes of time remaining, a brilliant header from Gareth Taylor secured the three points. It was to be the second game in a run of just one defeat in 21 matches and a run that propelled the Blues up the table.

The striker had only joined City in the November and says it was a big achievement for the club to have made the play-offs: "When I signed, we were around ninth or tenth in the league, something like that, and not really making a hell of a charge.

"My debut was against Luton and we drew 1-1 away from home," he says. The Blues went on to draw their next game (0-0 at home to Bristol Rovers) and lose the one after that (2-1 away at York). It was only really then that things changed.

"We had the Christmas period and the Wrexham game was huge," Taylor says. "As we did with all games, we took a massive support with us and I think that result was the one that got us moving. There was a hell of a downpour before and I always remember it being a bog of a pitch. It looked unlikely that the game would go ahead, but it did – and we went on to win 1-0 with a good goal from Gerard [Wiekens]."

"I'd had sporadic displays myself and I was in and out of the team... and, to be honest, on the morning of the game against Gillingham, I was really sweating on whether or not I'd even make the bench."

Up next was that match against Stoke where the centre forward scored his first goal for the club: "It was a big game," the striker remembers, "they were going for it as well that season. I actually had a goal disallowed just before I scored, which was a disappointment. But somebody showed it [the goal that stood] to me the other day on the video – Dicky's gone down the left side, cut back in and put a great cross over and I got my first goal, which was a fantastic feeling."

The run that saw the Blues make the Play-Off Final was something Taylor found himself in and out of the team for. But he says that didn't affect how he was feeling pre-match when the team were in the hotel in London. "I believe in fate and I thought, 'We're here for a reason'. We hadn't got that far to lose that day. But after 85 minutes I was thinking something different.

"There was a huge expectation on our shoulders. We had to do it. But the feeling [before the game] was pretty relaxed, to be honest. I can remember us all congregating in one room and discussing the game, talking about where we wanted to be and asking if we really wanted to be going back to places like Chesterfield or wherever, just over tea and biscuits.

"Little did we know that we were on the verge of double promotion

– which was a great achievement for that group of players, especially as, when we went up against Gillingham at Wembley, we didn't really tweak the team a lot. We only added a few names."

When it came to earning that first promotion, though, Taylor says he wasn't even sure if he was going to be a part of the team: "I'd had sporadic displays myself and I was in and out of the team. I came out of the team at the vital time in the build-up to Wembley and, to be honest, the morning of the game against Gillingham, I was really sweating on whether or not I'd even make the bench. There were only three subs in them days and, in the end, it was me, Ian Bishop and Tony Vaughan.

"So I was just filled with relief that I'd actually made the bench because I didn't think I was going to make it," he says. "I obviously had different emotions when I came on. Just after I came on, there was a goal kick to Gillingham and it was really direct – a ball down the middle and a goal. And I just thought, 'Jesus Christ, this isn't what you want coming on with three or four minutes left...'

"My parents were there and my wife was there that day," he continues. "Gillingham were celebrating. A lot of our fans had left the stadium. It was a surreal moment. The things we'd talked about and the things we'd wanted to do were just slipping away from us.

"I can remember both of our goals – I had a part to play in them both," he adds. "For the first, there was a bit of interchange in the Gillingham half and it was played in. I did a dummy and left it for Shaun [Goater], who had an opportunity and got tackled – and it broke to Kevin who put it in with a nice finish. But obviously then there were people who were just thinking it was a consolation.

"The next ball was a long diagonal," he continues, "I think it was from Gerard and I've managed to get above the defender and flick it on. Again Shaun nearly had a chance, but it fell to Paul and the rest is history.

"I'm not sure because I've not spoken to the rest of the players about that day, but I had an unbelievable feeling that it'd be ours," he says, "and you can just imagine how the Gillingham players were feeling when they were walking around after the whistle had gone and going into extra time they were so deflated. They'd just had it snatched away from them and we were in the ascendancy."

By that stage, though, as much as Gillingham were in defensive mode having switched formation to try and hold their 2-0 lead, City were in full on assault mode, too. "We had about four strikers on the pitch!" Taylor says. "Joe asked me to drop in and play in midfield – and I remember having so much of the ball in the extra time period. It was me and Bish [Ian Bishop] on a really big pitch and I really enjoyed it! I actually enjoyed playing in midfield and pulling the strings with Bish, even if extra time turned out to be a non-event.

"But when we got to penalties, I just remember going round to the lads and saying to them, 'This is ours... we haven't come this far to chuck it away now.' It was just a psychological thing, a feeling in my mind that we'd not done all that to lose on penalties."

The striker, though, never got the chance to take one of the kicks. Had the shootout gone on for long enough, then it would have got down to Taylor, but he wasn't listed as one of the first five – something he tells me he was a bit disappointed about: "I was actually on penalties earlier in the season," he says, "I missed one against Oldham at Maine Road. I actually scored in the game, but we lost 2-1 and I'd missed a penalty. I don't think Joe ever forgave me for that!"

The penalty came at 0-1 and would have been the equaliser. However, the miss let the Latics off the hook and they soon doubled their lead, before Taylor added the consolation with ten minutes left to play. It was City's first defeat in three months.

"It was a great period for me. I'd had my first child and I got married the Saturday after Wembley and a lot of the lads came to the wedding... The celebrations after Wembley are a bit sketchy, though..."

"So when he [Royle] was going around and marking the card for who was taking the penalties, I was looking at him as if to say, 'I'll have one,' but he sort of looked through me to see who else was putting their hand up. So I was disappointed not to take one, but it would have been really nerve-wracking – and the lads [that did take penalties] did their bit and so did Nicky Weaver.

"It was a great period for me," he says, "I'd had my first child – my first son – and I got married the Saturday after Wembley and a lot of the lads came to the wedding. So it was a great time.

"The celebrations after Wembley are a bit sketchy, though, because of the amount that was consumed," he says, laughing, "I actually remember going to Dicky's the day after for a barbeque. All of the guys were there and Chappy [kitman Les Chapman] was there.

"We had good guys around the club then," he continues, "the likes of Ronnie Evans [physio] – his lad George is in the academy now – or Roy Bailey [physio], Asa Hartford [reserve team coach], Willie Donachie [assistant manager], and obviously Joe. We had a good, solid staff in those days."

Taylor says that, throughout that season, there was pressure on the team to perform so that meant when it came to the final game of the campaign, the players were used to it. "I remember going to Blackpool and it just felt like a home game," he says, "we had three sides of the stadium almost. There were masses of pressure and if we hadn't played well, the fans would let us know about it. And there were some dark days, there's no doubt about that.

"But I always think," he continues, "if we hadn't have got back up [to Division One] that day, the club, with the amount of support that it had and has got, was always going to bounce back. People always say they might have fallen away, but I don't think so. Thankfully, we went up straight away and back-to-back, too.

"I wouldn't say the club was a sleeping giant back then because everyone knew how big it was, but the potential was always there and the fanbase was always there. So I think it was only a matter of time, really – if it hadn't been that season, or maybe even the season after, I think we would have got back there eventually."

Taylor didn't get as much game time as he would have liked the next year, spending large spells of the second half of the season on loan at Port Vale and Queens Park Rangers. "The following season," he says, "we were back in Division One and there were some big clubs in and around it. I played my part, but I didn't play as many games as I would have liked to have done personally."

The striker made 22 appearances for the club that season, though most were from the bench, and scored six goals. "I remember getting a couple against Portsmouth on a Tuesday night, and I scored at home – with the Goat – against Barnsley. So there were some good nights there, but the club was

> "I wouldn't say the club was a sleeping giant back then because everyone knew how big it was, but the potential was always there and the fanbase was always there. So I think it was only a matter of time, really – if it hadn't been that season... I think we would have got back there eventually."

moving on – the more success we had, I found we were signing strikers and I was struggling to get back into the team.

"I played my part and scored some important goals that got us promotion," he continues. "We had a system that was working and we had the same nucleus of players, and it was all about trusting each other and doing the business. We didn't go up as champions, but to go up in that tense game at Ewood Park was unbelievable, really."

Looking at the present day, however, and a few fans may be surprised to find out that Taylor is back at Manchester City. About a year before contacting the players I needed to interview for this book, I was invited down to a charity game at Platt Lane to interview some former players for the radio show *Blue Moon Live* on Imagine FM. It was while I was there that I spotted Taylor playing for the Platt Lane Staff team – in a friendly against the Former Players XI.

It turned out that he's now the head coach of the Under-16s side.

"I've been back here two years," he says, "I'm also the 12-16s co-ordinator at the academy, so I take care of the coaches for the players within that age bracket. And it's fantastic for me. I love working with the players and I'm working in a place that I know really well, because this [Platt Lane] is where I trained as a first team player.

"We've got the new academy that's currently being built that we'll be moving to soon," he says of the plans for the developments near the Etihad Stadium (which, at the time of writing, are being constructed), "and it's funny because I struggle sometimes to compare the club that I played for to what it is now.

"Before I was Under-16s coach, I was working on a scheme called the Rishworth Project, which involved an exchanged programme between boys from Abu Dhabi and here. I had numerous visits to the UAE and, seeing how things work out there, you can see the vision that the owners have for this club and the quest for excellence, I'd say. They really want everything to be spot on and I think when you go there, that really hits home.

"It's great for me to be working in this environment," he says. "I've got the experience of what it's like to play for this club, which I think is important. And I'm really enjoying it. I played until I was 38 or 39 and to have that seamless transition into coaching was one that I'm really thankful for.

"Back when I was playing, it would have been easier for a young player to break into the first team than it would be now," he adds. "Obviously, the bar's really been raised. But we're about developing the person here, not just the player. That's really key and it's an avenue I tend to go down a bit with the players."

Taylor tells me that he can – but rarely does – speak to first team players in his new role. However, he says that he has to laugh when outsiders say the comeback that saw City win the league in 2012 was a once-in-a-lifetime thing: "I was in the stadium with my wife and children that day," he says. "It was another unbelievable moment, really – I went through all the emotions like every fan did.

"I actually turned to my wife and said, 'I know how you felt now at Wembley.' It was horrible for me watching it, but I think if you're involved out on the pitch, you're not feeling that tension and that emotion. It's obviously in your mind that you're up against it and need to do something, but you *can* do something about it. When you're in the stands, you can't.

"My youngest son is 10 and he's a huge City fan, so just the emotion of lifting him up in the air at full time [in the game with QPR in May 2012]... I know how the fans in 1999 felt now."

13 Tony Vaughan

Tony Vaughan was one of the players I was worried about tracking down when the interviews for this book began. A Google search of him found that the internet didn't really know what had happened to the defender when he'd finished his playing career. His Wikipedia page ends with him working for Audi in their showroom in Lincoln, but when I emailed their office I discovered he had moved on. He had recently been interviewed on the radio, but contacting the journalist that recorded it proved fruitless, too.

However, by sheer coincidence, I was invited as a member of the press to Les Chapman's testimonial game at Boundary Park. The game was made up of two teams of former City players, with the club's kitman on the 'home' side. On the 'away' side and playing at left back was Tony Vaughan.

City Career Stats

Apps: 72 (6 sub)
Goals: 2

Signed: August 1997
Left: March 2000

Debut: Portsmouth (h), 1997
Result: 2-2 draw

"When we all walked out, I ended up being next to Joe [Royle]," Vaughan says, talking about the testimonial game, "we were waiting for Chappy to come out and we were looking for our families in the stand. I got talking to Joe about when Andy Morrison was walking down the line at Wembley [the captain was introducing his team to the game's guests of honour for the day].

"When the national anthems came on Joe looked at me and asked me how I knew the words," he continues, "and I pointed at the big screen inside Wembley and said, 'They're written up there!'"

Vaughan didn't start in the game in 1999. Named as one of the substitutes, he joined the action in the second half just after the hour mark, replacing an injured Andy Morrison. At the time, it was goalless and around 20 minutes later the Blues were losing. I ask him if it's difficult to join a game as important as that one was when it's already an hour old.

"I think you can tell from the two goals," he says, laughing. "I've never watched the whole game back, but I think I was involved in both of their goals. You could say that was through coming on and not being fully on it from the start. I think it was one of those things – Andy [Morrison] had taken an injection before the game and I think he was starting to struggle a bit, so the gaffer put me on."

Even though the defender knew that he was beginning the match on the bench, he tells me that – before the game – he was excited: "It was a big occasion and we'd worked hard all year to get to there. We thought we'd get promoted without going through the play-offs, but obviously it didn't happen. I was excited, but I was a bit disappointed as well because I wasn't starting.

"Joe had told me a couple of days before that I wasn't going to be playing," he continues, "I had time to get rid of the disappointment. It was a big game and it's a team game, so even though you're not playing, you still want your mates to do well and you still want the team to get promoted. So we all rallied round.

"In the end, it was one of those days that happened in a flash. You look back and try to remember it, but things only come back to you every now and again. It was a blur."

Vaughan puts the comeback down to the influence that one member of the coaching staff had with the team. Carl Asaba's opening goal came with nine

> "We were always taught to play until the final whistle and when Carl Asaba scored, we had that 'never say die' attitude. I think that showed with the way the game ended up..."

minutes of time to play, while Robert Taylor doubled that advantage six minutes later. More often than not, that situation means it's game over – but May 1999 was one of the occasions where the unlikely happened. And that, Vaughan thinks, was because of the assistant manager.

"Willie Donachie used a lot of mental and psychological techniques with us," he says. "We were always taught to play until the final whistle and when Carl Asaba scored, we had that 'never say die' attitude. I think that showed with the way the game ended up, so when he scored we always knew that we could score goals. Obviously, it's disappointing to concede, but it was that attitude that got us through to penalties.

"The game is 90 minutes – or 95 minutes, however long the referee plays," he continues, "you've always got the opportunity to get down the other end and nick a goal. Fortunately, Kevin Horlock scored and then Dicky got his, too.

"When Kev scored, the fourth official put the board up to say there was an extra five minutes. Because Willie had instilled into us that you play until the end, I think that in a lot of the games that season we did score late goals. And every game we played was like everybody's cup final – we took

"I remember finding [when Dickov scored the equaliser] that Wembley's a long pitch to go and run after somebody..."

thousands of fans everywhere we went and we were playing away games like home games because the City fans were everywhere. So we'd learnt to give everything until the end that season.

"I remember finding [when Dickov scored the equaliser] that Wembley's a long pitch to go and run after somebody," he says with a smile. "They took Carl Asaba off thinking they'd won and maybe that was the wrong decision by their manager. Maybe he should have kept him on. But it gave us that little bit of a boost.

"It was all one-way traffic in extra time. I remember thinking we were on top for most of it. I think we had all the play, but just couldn't score. I remember it being attack, attack, attack – but we just couldn't get past Vince Bartram. We should have gone on to win it in extra time, it shouldn't have got to penalties. But eventually we got there."

The fans weren't as confident as perhaps some of the players were at 2-0, with many of them leaving the stadium and beginning the journey home. "I don't remember them leaving and coming back in," Vaughan says, "but I read about it afterwards. I can remember, though, when Nicky Weaver saved the penalty and we all ran after him – that celebration with the fans is something that will never go away. I'm getting goose pimples now thinking about it and it makes your hair stand up. It was amazing."

That brings us on to the topic of penalties. Vaughan remained on the halfway line throughout the shootout, with Shaun Goater down to take the fifth – the kick that wasn't needed in the end. Vaughan, though, says he would have volunteered if he were needed: "I would have taken one if it had got to it. I wasn't in the first five, but if it got there, I wouldn't have had a problem taking one – luckily I didn't have to!

"I think, for me, the most memorable was Dicky's," he says. "We'd practised in little goals on Maine Road the day before, and Dicky was smashing them past Nicky Weaver left, right and centre. Everyone would have put their mortgage on him scoring, so for him to hit both posts and it not go in was incredible. He'd have been the one person you'd have expected to score. But the lads took the penalties well and luckily for us we went on to win."

Talk of the comeback at Wembley sways the conversation towards what happened at the Etihad Stadium in May 2012. When Martin Tyler swore that "you'll never see anything like this ever again", he was forgetting that City fans had been there, done it, bought the t-shirt.

"I think City fans know," Vaughan says, "that City never do anything the easy way. It's always been that they leave everything to the last minute. I actually said [in 2012] that they'd probably win the league in the last minute – I wish I'd put a bet on it now! I said that I could see them coming back and scoring in injury time like what happened at Wembley, but to win the Premier League."

The game at Wembley was something of a preview of the emotions the fans would go through 13 years later. From despair, through to hope, through to elation – the supporters didn't have it easy. Vaughan, though, believes that the Premier League title under Roberto Mancini might not have been possible had the club not come back to win in the Play-Off Final in 1999.

"City fans know that City never do anything the easy way. It's always been that they leave everything to the last minute."

"People always say to you, 'Where would the club have been if we didn't win that game?' and it's one of them that you just don't know," he says. "We won the game and kicked on, winning promotion straight after and those back-to-back promotions got us to the Premier League. You can't really say where the club would be now without coming back that year, so it was a big game."

I ask him if he or any of the other players were feeling the pressure before the match – with rumours coming out afterwards that the club was in a very difficult financial situation. Vaughan says he wasn't aware of anything off the pitch, and once more put that down to Willie Donachie's psychology techniques.

"All we were bothered about was playing for 90 minutes or 95 minutes, however long it was until the whistle went. Luckily, we all had that strong mentality and that strong attitude, so even when we went two goals down, we were able to stick together and get the result that all the City fans and we wanted."

The unity at the club at that time is something that all the players from the team speak about. After years of various people at City swimming in all directions, the Blues were suddenly coming together and all pushing the same way. Vaughan says that everybody in the dressing room was fighting for each other.

"Without being disrespectful to anybody, there were no superstars in the team," he says, "we were all hard, solid, working lads. We all grafted for each other – if one got hit, the next one would come in and help them out. We backed each other in tackles. If it all went off on the pitch or if it went off in the tunnel, we'd back each other up. We'd win together and we'd lose together. That's the spirit we had."

Vaughan had been in the City team for much of the run-up to the Play-Off Final, and featured in both legs of the semi-final against Wigan. In fact, in the first game, he had the chance to equalise for the Blues – who had been a goal down since the first minute. Vaughan had actually taken the throw in that Gerard Wiekens and Nicky Weaver both left, so technically got the assist for Stuart Barlow's goal, though no blame could fall on the defender's shoulders. In the second half, a loose ball broke his way, but – with the entire goal to aim at – the defender's wild swing with his right foot sent the effort skewing wide. He begins to smile when I bring it up.

"My gaffer [where he now works] is a massive City fan," he says, "and he's had it up on YouTube. It was just a complete swinger. I would have been better not bothering and just giving it back to the goalkeeper! My right foot was only ever for standing on... It wasn't the best."

Vaughan left City in 2000 after struggling to break his way back into the first team following loan spells at Cardiff and Nottingham Forest. He was transferred to Forest, before moving on to Mansfield and Barnsley. He then finished his career in non-league with Hucknall Town.

"I've got no regrets," he says about his career, "I've done what every little boy dreams of doing. I've played for my home town team, I've played in every league – including the Scottish Premier League [in a loan spell at Motherwell, while he was at Nottingham Forest]. I've lived my dream.

"I'm now working in form concrete," he continues, "I've been doing that for a couple of years now. Once you come out of football, it's not going to guarantee you a job – even if you go into coaching. You either need to know somebody or be lucky to have someone bring you in [for a coaching role]. It's not that easy for ex-footballers to get into the coaching game – there's a lot of written work, but that's not for me. Give me a bag of balls and some bibs and I'll be able to put on a session, but get me to write it all down and it's not my cup of tea.

"Fortunately for me now, my gaffer's a City fan. He was playing golf in a legends day and I was there. We got talking and he offered me the job – now the rest is history, as they say.

"I retired in the 2005-06 season," he continues. "Obviously, you find it difficult to get work once you've retired – your phone stops ringing, people don't want to know you because you're not a footballer any more, and it can be a hard life. I can understand why some people slip into depression.

"Footballers nowadays are multimillionaires and they don't have to worry about when they retire," he says, "or they put money away or they've done this or done that. But for people who don't make millions and haven't got any qualifications, it's difficult when you do come out of the game. You don't get that much help from people, so I battled along.

"I fell on a job at Lincoln Audi about two years after being out of the game," he says – and it's here I tell him that I tried to contact him through them and he remembers an old friend telling him that somebody was trying to get in touch. "It was last-one-in-first-one-out at Audi and around that time I lost my dad, too.

"That changed my life completely. It brought me back to Manchester – I came back with two bin bags of possessions and started my life again. It's

> "I tried to do my coaching badges, but I felt like they were putting hurdles in front of us and they shouldn't be... Instead, they're bringing people into the game who can do the written work, but have never played in front of 30-odd thousand people."

only in the last year or so that I've started reading the newspaper again, listening to the radio or even watching football on TV again. I'd done it for so long that I fell out of love with it.

"I tried to do my coaching badges, but I felt like they were putting hurdles in front of us and they shouldn't be," he says, "they should be trying to get ex-pros to stay in the game and help the youngsters. Instead, they're bringing people into the game who can do the written work, but have never played in front of 30-odd thousand people. They've never been there and done it, but they can talk the talk because they can write things down on a piece of paper.

"Now, though, I'm going to work every day with a smile on my face," he says about his new career, "I'm working with a great bunch of lads and the gaffer's good as gold. It's just like being in a football club again because the banter is just like it was in the dressing room. It's a small-knit company and we're all together."

When I met Tony for the first time at Edgeley Park, he was holding the hand of his little lad, Dexter. Before we finish, I have to ask if he's any aspirations of following in his father's footsteps.

"At the minute he's a bit of a golfer!" Vaughan replies, "he can kick a ball and can kick it well – at this moment in time, he could probably kick it as high into the Kippax as I used to be able to and he's only three! If he wants to go down the football route, without blowing my own trumpet, he couldn't have anyone better to support him. I've gone from being a young boy wanting to be a footballer and making it, so if he wants to go down that route, I'll help him as much as I can."

14 IAN BISHOP
Midfielder (substitute)

"I remember Joe Royle coming onto the field and saying to me, 'You changed the game.' I replied, 'Yeah, when I came on it was 0-0... then after I came one we went 2-0 down... I did change the game!'"

I'm sitting with Ian Bishop in the bar at Reddish Blues supporters' club meeting. He's visiting the UK from the United States, where he now lives – and the interview for this chapter of the book has been split between his flying visit home and via email. It's in the bar that he tells me he should probably have never played at Wembley for City, given the situation that he was in when the club qualified for the play-offs.

CITY CAREER STATS

Apps: 117 (34 sub)
Goals: 7

Signed: August 1989, March 1998
Left: December 1989, March 2001

First Debut: Liverpool (a), 1989
Result: 3-1 defeat

Second Debut: Bradford (a), 1998
Result: 2-1 defeat

"I wasn't supposed to play," he says, "I got injured in the final league game, I think it was York at home. I tore a hamstring and the specialist said it would take six weeks to get right. I was having none of that as the final, if we got there, was around three weeks away. I had to train and convince Joe [Royle] that I was ok to play.

"My one and only Wembley appearance and I wasn't supposed to be there!" he continues. "Missing the two Wigan games was bad enough. I did have the pleasure of watching the away leg in the Kippax on the big screen with the fans though, which was nerve-wracking in itself.

"The week before the final, I decided to train. I thought if I could prove my fitness then I would make at least a squad place. I must admit now that I sort of conned my way through training that week by protecting myself against anything that would extend my hamstring in any way. I think the only person I was conning was myself, though, because Joe saw right through me.

"I had a long chat with him at the end of the week and he told me that he couldn't take the risk of starting me, which I totally agreed with because no matter what it means to the individual, the team comes first, and I understood that. He was not even going to have me on the bench. He was worried that I'd come on and break down, especially if we had to play extra time.

"Even on the day before we left, he said he wasn't going to risk it and I had to beg him – I said, 'I've got to be there. I don't care if it's on the bench or not, but I've got to be there.' I don't know what it was that finally convinced him but I got my wish."

Bishop joined the action with 30 minutes of the match remaining, as part of a double substitution – he and Tony Vaughan replaced Michael Brown and Andy Morrison. He tells me that he wasn't expecting to be involved for as long as he was.

"I remember that we weren't too convincing in the first half, but didn't expect to be called upon so early. Joe felt that we weren't moving the ball as we knew we could and I suppose possession was key on a pitch like Wembley. He told me to get us passing and create."

As we had touched on earlier, not long after Bishop had joined the game, the Blues were two goals behind. As the game began to get stretched, Gillingham took two opportunities that presented themselves – both after the 80 minute mark – and it looked like City would be facing another slog in Division Two the following season. However, the midfielder says he didn't once lose confidence.

"I never thought it was over," Bishop says, "we were the better team. You never think about that when you're on the field. I remember playing for West Ham in 1992 when we beat Manchester United 1-0, when Leeds won the title, and [Sir Alex] Ferguson had a go at us in his book. He said our performance was 'obscene' and asked how a team that was already relegated could do that, saying that it was just because it was Manchester United. But that's bullshit. You play to win and until that last whistle goes – unless the game's 4-0 or something like that – you're in with a chance.

> "I was conscious of my hamstring. The last thing I wanted was to do was to come on and have to go off again and leave us a man down. But I conned my way through training, so I thought I'd con my way through the game as well!"

"2-0's a dangerous scoreline anyway," he continues, "you're never done at 2-0. If a team scores one back, they get the momentum and the other team is on the back foot. That seemed to be what happened – I'd like to think I played a big part in that day. I still ended up having to play an hour!

"I was conscious of my hamstring. The last thing I wanted to do was to come on and have to go off again and leave us a man down. But I conned my way through training, so I thought I'd con my way through the game as well!" he says with a chuckle. There's something about his sense of humour that is typically Scouse – both delightfully cheeky and yet somehow charming.

We begin to talk about the two goals. "I thought we had played better in the second half. Kev's goal came from a decent passing move that ended up being blocked – he followed up and slotted it in low. There were still bodies that it could have hit, but he found the gap.

"As for Dicky's goal," he continues, "I remember it took the last bit of breath out of my body at the time, and I haven't experienced a feeling like it since. I still say how jealous I am of him. Not only of scoring the goal itself, but I think that the picture of him sliding on his knees after the goal is one of the best you will see. If you wanted to ask any of the players how they feel about that day, then his face says it all. It couldn't have happened to a better person, too. He deserves all of my jealousy."

After such late drama, it was natural that nothing happened in extra time – with both teams perhaps a little too wary of losing the game than actually pushing on to win it. So, with the game having gone to penalties, I ask Bishop if he had any plans to take one. "No," he says, before adding, "I said to the boys, 'I've had enough glory here today, you can go and get some!'"

However, when it comes to the spot-kicks, Bishop thinks he has a claim to fame. "Now everyone who takes penalties," he says, "the whole team is on the halfway line with their arms around each other. I got everybody together that day and I think that's the first time it ever happened."

I must look at him dubiously at this point in the interview because he begins

> "I still say how jealous I am of him [Dickov]... If you wanted to ask any of the players how they feel about that day, then his face says it all. It couldn't have happened to a better person, too. He deserves all of my jealousy."

to smile and says, "Honestly, I'm not kidding. I may be wrong, but I think that's the first time." And here I must confess to trying to find photographic evidence of it having happened before that 1999 Play-Off Final – I wasn't able to spot anything with various Google searches. It might not conclusively prove that Bishop was the first player to get his team to do it, but, in the circumstances, we'll give it to him for now.

"I remember pulling the boys together and telling them that no matter what happened, we had already done ourselves and the club proud. The thought of taking one was not in my or the gaffer's mind to be honest. To tell you the truth, I was amazed that I had got through the second half and thirty minutes extra time with my hamstring intact. I would love to tell you that I wanted to take the fifth one and would have dinked it down the middle, but I would be lying. I will say though that we all had the utmost confidence in Weaves."

"I just jumped on the train... I found a seat and got myself a couple of beers. It wasn't a seat with a table, so I put my beers on the pull down tray and kept my head down... until one person stopped right next to me. I looked up and saw the groundsman from Platt Lane..."

Following the game, the players and coaches travelled home and celebrated with a barbeque at Paul Dickov's house. Bishop, however, remained in London with his family. The midfielder remembers it clearly.

"After the game, we had some celebratory drinks in the hotel near the stadium. My wife and kids were staying in London for the bank holiday. Our good friends and old next-door neighbours were at the game and we had planned a nice celebration in London that night. I did feel that I should have gone back on the team bus with the boys, and I was going to miss a barbecue at Dicky's the following day. All of the staff were going to be there and I was missing out on it.

"We went out with friends in London that night, but I couldn't stop wondering what the lads were up to. My wife kept asking if I was ok, but I didn't want to be there. The next day, which was the morning of the barbecue, we had planned to take the kids for lunch. I asked my wife if she would mind if I jumped on a train to be with the boys and she said that's where I belonged and she'd drive the kids back home the next day.

"I got a taxi to Euston," he continues, "the train was at two and I was going to miss it. I arrived so late that I didn't have time to buy a ticket. I just jumped on the train and thought I would buy the ticket in transit. I found a seat and got myself a couple of beers. It wasn't a seat with a table so I put my beers on the pull down tray and kept my head down.

"After a short while, I started to notice there was a lot of people going by in City colours. I sort of kept myself to myself until one person stopped right next to me. I looked up and saw the groundsman from Platt Lane, who told me that there were four coaches filled with City fans further down. That was it. I went to the buffet car and bought two trays of beers and set off down the train.

"The further I got, the more fans started singing and chanting my name. I opened this one door and I couldn't move. There were people in the luggage racks, swinging off tables, and the carriage was bouncing. I didn't sit down for the whole journey. It was the best train ride you could ever wish for. I saw the ticket guard open the door to the carriage and turn back, so I never did pay for a ticket.

"If I remember rightly, I got off the train at Macclesfield, and was going to get a taxi to Bowden until one of the fans said that his dad was picking him up and he would be happy to take me to Dicky's house. I was eternally grateful to him and his dad.

"I got outside the house," he says, "and I shouted Dicky's name. He leapt over his garden fence, which was taller than him, and pinned me down on the front lawn."

The Play-Off Final came quite early on in Bishop's second spell with Manchester City. The midfielder re-joined the Blues in March 1998, a couple of months before they were relegated to Division Two, having originally left in 1989. Bishop came through the ranks in the early '80s at Everton and, following spells at Carlisle and Bournemouth, joined City for just under half a million pounds.

"When I left Everton at 19, I'd made my debut there – which was 20 brief minutes. I felt like my full debut was my first game for Manchester City at Anfield," he says. "It was the biggest move for me because it brought me back into the top flight. I wanted to get back there – I'd had four years at Carlisle, where I'd slumped down to the bottom of the fourth division, but I believed in myself that I was better than that.

"I moved to Bournemouth and I think it may have had a lot to do with that second-last game of the season that solidified my move to Manchester," he says. City had been three goals up at half time, thanks to two strikes from Paul Moulden and one from Trevor Morley. But a

"When Howard [Kendall] came to City, I said to Paul Lake, 'It's been nice knowing you!' and he said to me that it [a transfer] couldn't happen. But I had a feeling it would."

turnaround in the second half, inspired by Bishop, helped the Cherries to an unlikely 3-3 draw.

"I'd actually played at Maine Road for Carlisle, as well," he says. "I scored, too – we beat City 3-1 and I scored a header. When I scored a header against Man United [in the 5-1 win at Maine Road in 1989], people said I didn't score headers – but they obviously didn't remember! I looked a little bit different in them days, too.

"But Maine Road was the place for me," he says, "the hotchpotch stands, being out there and playing, the Kippax, and the atmosphere, it was fantastic."

Bishop's first spell with City didn't last very long. In fact, he made only 24 appearances for the club before he was sold to West Ham, where he went on to play the majority of his career. Some say the writing was on the wall for the midfielder as soon as Howard Kendall replaced Mel Machin – the manager that signed him. Kendall had previously sold Bishop when he was managing at Everton.

"I've spoken to Howard and to Lou Macari [West Ham manager at the time] about what went on," he says. "Obviously, as a player, you don't get the full story. The club want money – or, in that case, Howard wanted a player [West Ham's Mark Ward] – and Lou told me afterwards that he didn't want Ward to leave. So he thought, when Howard asked who he wanted [from City], if he said he wanted me then the deal would be off and Howard wouldn't let me go.

"And, as we know, Howard *did* let me go," he continues. "Lou said to me that he couldn't believe Howard had done that and he said he felt he'd got the better end of the deal.

"When Howard came to City, I said to Paul Lake, 'It's been nice knowing you!' and he said to me that it [a transfer] couldn't happen. But I had a feeling it would. Howard had let me go through no fall-out at Everton. I had nine months of my contract left and he told me Carlisle had come in. He kept the sell-on clause, so he obviously rated me as a player, but my way through to the first team at Everton was blocked by tonnes of players he'd brought in when he took over the job.

"When he came in to City, he had a job to do," Bishop continues. "He wanted to keep them up and at the time maybe he needed someone who was more of a battling player than I was. I'm a big believer that you can play your way out of anything. Maybe he thought Mark Ward would do a job for him and he was prepared to let me go – and, at the end of the day, he kept City up that season, so whatever decisions he made then were possibly – not probably – the right ones.

"It changed my life," he says. "First of all, it was upheaval again – I'd just moved from the south coast back up north and then it was back down south. It was chaos really, I couldn't have gone much further: Carlisle to Bournemouth to Manchester to London. But I wouldn't change it for the world and it had an effect on my life. Things happen for a reason."

During Bishop's short first spell with City, he was part of the team that would earn one of the club's biggest and most memorable Manchester derby wins. In September 1989, the newly promoted Blues hosted the Reds and went on to win 5-1, in a game later dubbed the Maine Road Massacre. Bishop scored the third goal that afternoon, adding to two strikes from David Oldfield, and one each from Trevor Morley and Andy Hinchcliffe.

"I think it was Paul Ince who was alongside me and he just didn't track my run... I must have deceived him with my pace. He probably didn't realise someone could run that slowly!"

Going into the match, Bishop tells me he wasn't expecting the result: "You never believe you're going to get your arse kicked," he says, "but you never believe you're going to trounce them 5-1, either. We were a young team, they were a team full of superstars and we were fired up. To stop and think about it now, I'd probably get the same feelings in my stomach as I did before the game.

"That game will never go away," he continues. "When you come back to the club – which I haven't done very often – and look around, people are still talking about it. It's a part of my life and the club's history and I'm just proud to have been a part of that."

I ask him if he can remember the header, to which Bishop laughs: "Of course I do," he says, "I watch it every other day! When it happened, I didn't realise how far I'd run. I remember when Stevie Redmond broke the attack up on the edge of our penalty area and I was more or less standing next to him. I think it was Paul Ince who was alongside me and he just didn't track my run... I must have deceived him with my pace. He probably didn't realise someone could run that slowly!

"Trevor Morley was behind me and he was going to have a go at me because I didn't leave it for him," he continues, "I just threw myself at it. I knew I was going to have to dive for it. I didn't know what was going to happen afterwards – I ended up upside down – and Jim Leighton [United's goalkeeper] was sliding out. I didn't see it go in. If you look at the video, once I've heard the roar, I've had a look up to try and see where the ball was and there was a delay before I started running away.

"I didn't know what celebration to do because I wasn't used to celebrating. I didn't score that many. I talked about Dicky's photo about him sliding on his knees, I think that picture of Paul Lake picking me up with my fist in the air is just as famous."

Bishop was away from Maine Road for almost a decade before he returned when the club had fallen on hard times. "I had an agreement with Harry [Redknapp]. I had nine years at West Ham and they'd offered me another year with a testimonial, but I didn't like what was happening there. I wasn't his favourite at the time, we'd had fall-outs and what have you – I felt I should have been playing and he had me on the bench. It was something like 23 games that season

> "I wouldn't have left West Ham for any other club. I wouldn't have given up a testimonial for any other club. And I didn't care what division it was..."

and I'd only got on the field I think three times, so I said to him, 'I'm 32 years old, I need to be playing.'

"I asked him if he would give me a free transfer so I could sort out a move," he continues, "the club wouldn't have to pay anything, but I'd give up a testimonial year – which was massive: I could have got a lot of tax-free money! But the thing that was important for me was to play – I wanted to play for West Ham, I didn't want to leave. I'd had opportunities to go. I think I could have gone to QPR two or three times, Brian Clough wanted me at Forest I think twice, Southampton had come in... and I turned it all down. I didn't want to leave the club.

"I was out in London and my wife called me and said, 'You have to come home right now,' – but to be fair, she always says that and I never normally listen to her! She said I'd had a phone call from Mick McGuire from the PFA, who was one of Joe [Royle]'s friends. I called him back and he told me Joe wanted to speak to me, so I immediately thought, 'Oh, Jesus, it's City.'

"I wouldn't have left West Ham for any other club," he says, "I wouldn't have given up a testimonial for any other club. And I didn't care what division it was – I knew they were on their way down because there was only something like five games left. It still could have been salvaged, but it didn't matter to me.

"I spoke to Joe and drove straight up there. I think they were playing Port Vale with the reserves. I met him at Maine Road, agreed everything straight away and then I phoned Harry and told him that I'd signed. It wasn't a proper transfer. It wasn't the right way to go about things, but I reminded him that he'd shaken my hand on the training field one day and said if I found a club he'd let me have a free transfer. He wanted to argue about it, but I told him it was too late and it was done. I told him that I'd be out of his hair and this was where I wanted to be, so he told me, 'If that's what you want, then ok.'

"The City I'd left was different. Even though results hadn't gone our way that year, we were playing some good stuff and people were talking about us. When I came back, it was like *Midnight Express* – when he arrives at the asylum and they're all walking around in a circle in the same way. There were 54 players at that club walking the same way, and I decided to walk the other way.

"I didn't want to be a part of that," he continues, "I knew some of the players who were languishing there on big money and I couldn't not be their friend. But I didn't want to hear the bad stuff they wanted to say about the club. I'd just arrived and I wanted to help the club. I mixed in with the people who I thought wanted the club to succeed and, even though we did go down that year, we did succeed.

"People say you should never go back, but from the two spells I had at the club, I have nothing but great memories, great stories and I met some great people."

For Bishop, the second promotion he enjoyed with City had eerie reminders of the first. He was named on the bench for the final game of the season at Blackburn and came on in the second

> "The City I'd left was different... When I came back, it was like *Midnight Express* – when he arrives at the asylum and they're all walking around in a circle the same way. There were 54 players at that club walking the same way, and I decided to walk the other way."

half. This time, though, the Blues were already losing – when they needed to draw to secure second place in the league.

"It was weird," he says, "my best memory of that day was that there were more fans outside than there were in the stadium. I nearly died that day, too! When the supporters ran on the field at full time, I got trampled and couldn't get up. People were trying to take my shirt, my shorts, my boots... and I was picked up left, right and centre. I thought I was going to get smothered!

"It was another day that I don't really remember a lot about the next morning," he says, grinning cheekily, "it's a good job you watch the video though, eh?"

Back in the Premier League, though, Bishop struggled to hold down a first team place: "I didn't get as many starts as I would have liked. I know my age came into it," he says. For that top-flight season under Royle, Bishop was 35. "It was awkward for me, because if I started I was told I was the best player out there, but the next game I'd be on the bench. And if I came off the bench, I was told I changed the game, but wouldn't start the next one.

"I would have really loved to have stayed at the club and see out my playing days there and join in a coaching capacity," he continues, "but it was difficult when I wasn't playing as much as I wanted to be. The time came around March when an offer from the United States came up and I thought that over there I could play another three or four years.

"I still think I could have played in the Premier League at 36 or 37. I was never fast, so I couldn't lose my pace! Your speed is your speed of thought. [Ryan] Giggs and [Paul] Scholes did it and I think I could have done it, too."

However, as much as there was a huge difference between the club that Bishop left in 1989 and rejoined nine years later, there's been an even bigger change between the one he left again in 2001 and what it is today. The former midfielder says he's happy for the fans.

"It couldn't have happened to a better club. I've seen the suffering, I know about the suffering, and I've been part of it. I just think that it's a godsend that it's come here now and what happened in May 2012. People ask if I wished I'd been involved, but my regret is that I was on my own watching it in Florida. Even if I were just a spectator or just watching it in a pub here, at least I'd have got the feeling of it all.

"Don't get me wrong, I was still jumping up and down on the couch, but my celebrations only went on for a day and it probably went on all summer here."

There's one final thing I need to ask Bishop about and it's something that many will find surprising. The ex-City player wasn't just a footballer, but he was also an author – writing a series of children's books that, at the time of the interview, have never been published.

"I was doing it while I was still playing," he says. "When we had our first child in 1992, I started painting pictures on the bedroom walls. We had our second child in 1995 and our third in 1998. Then I was reading them stories at bedtime and there were no kids' books about football.

"I used to like to draw and so I decided to invent a team of characters that I named and gave them double meanings with football clichés," he explains. "I liked writing it and I think grown-ups would have read into the double-meanings, but the kids would like them for the characters. So I thought the parents reading and the kids would both get a bit of enjoyment out of it.

"I got offered a publishing deal in 2000 and I turned it down. I'd completed five of the ten books, but the other five were finished in my head anyway so it was just a case of putting them down on paper. And that's when the move to Miami came up..."

"I got offered a publishing deal in 2000 and I turned it down. I'd completed five of the ten books, but the other five were finished in my head anyway so it was just a case of putting them down on paper. And that's when the move to Miami came up – I turned the publishing deal down and took the move and then forgot about it."

As we finish the interview, I ask if he has any plans to finish the books. "You know what," he says, "I wouldn't mind speaking to somebody about doing a little animated film. I've still got the ideas there. I'd better get them down on paper before I forget them completely, though."

15 JOE ROYLE

Manager

I pulled up outside Joe Royle's house with about an hour to go before the interview. I'm notoriously bad at timekeeping, so I made sure that I arrived with plenty to spare – having set off early in case of bad traffic or in case I got lost or something like that. I figured an hour was too early to knock on his door, so I sat in the car and played Peggle on my phone.

I waited and waited, and the time just seemed to slowly tick around towards the agreed hour. In the end, I decided to knock on his front door around ten minutes early – that, I deemed, was acceptable. But there was no answer.

I went back to the car and waited some more. While I was there, nobody pulled into his driveway and I didn't see anybody walk in through the gates either, but nevertheless I returned at the agreed time and knocked once more, just in case he'd been in the garden or hadn't heard my first knock. But still there was no answer.

I waited a bit longer, tried once more and then phoned his mobile – which went straight through to voicemail. I was beginning to get worried. Instead of sitting in the car, I was now pacing up and down the road, trying to decide what I should do.

CITY MANAGERIAL STATS

Games: 171
Wins: 74 (43.27%)
Draws: 47 (27.49%)
Defeats: 50 (29.24%)

Goals For: 261
Goals Against: 192

Signed: February 1998
Left: May 2001

First Game: Ipswich (h), 1998
Result: 2-1 defeat

Shortly after, Joe called me and apologised for not being home. He was in Preston, at a match that had been set up so an overseas player could have a trial. He had emailed to explain we needed to re-arrange the interview – as he had had a problem with his phone and lost my number – but the email had bounced into my spam filter and, unfortunately, I hadn't seen it.

We re-arranged and I was back at his house exactly a week later.

"...he [Ian Bishop] laughs about it because I'd previously credited him with changing us – and he did, because he got us passing the ball again. But he did change the game because he went on at 0-0 and then we went 2-0 down!"

"It was pure Manchester City," the former manager says to me about the Play-Off Final. "I was feeling confident. We'd won at Gillingham and, quite honestly, I thought we were the team in form. We'd finished the season very strongly to the point where, at one stage, it looked like there was a chance of automatic promotion. But, given our position prior to Christmas, I suppose the play-offs were great to have.

"I was just hoping that those who can do, do on the day," he continues. "You're looking for your best players to perform. For instance, it was a blow Bish [Ian Bishop] didn't start. It was unfortunate because I'd wanted him to miss the league game previous to it, where he picked up a hamstring injury, but the bugger wouldn't listen. I think he was suspicious that if we'd played well and won without him then he wouldn't play in the play-offs. So I adhered to his wishes and, of course, he did his hamstring.

"I wanted him on the pitch as soon as I could, really," he says, "and he laughs about it because I'd previously credited him with changing us – and he did, because he got us passing the ball again. But he did change the game because he went on at 0-0 and then we went 2-0 down!"

The ex-manager laughs as he re-tells the story. "But quite seriously," he continues, "he had an influence on the team and he had respect that was always going to be a big part of the day. He got us passing the ball – we'd been ok, but we hadn't been anywhere near our best.

"One or two of the younger players maybe froze a bit on the day, Andy Morrison was struggling with a knee problem, and I felt happier when Bish came on," the manager says.

Despite City being just on top for most of the game and creating the better chances, the Blues suddenly found themselves two goals behind with only a few minutes to play.

"I remember turning to Willie Donachie and saying, 'It looks like Scunny next season,'" Royle explains, with Scunthorpe having won promotion in the Division Three Play-Off Final at Wembley the day before. "Not that there's anything wrong with Scunthorpe, but it was just the way I was feeling.

"Of course, the goal from Kevin Horlock changed it and the fourth official put five minutes up," he adds. "Asa [Hartford] was the first to spot it. He came running down and told me and the whole thing just grew from there. In pure City style, they'd taken their striker off to try and kill the game and I was convinced that, in extra time, we were going to do it. I thought we had the impetus and had the upper hand to go on and win it, but we didn't.

"When Kevin scored, I can't say I felt like we'd do it," he continues, "but I wasn't feeling negative because I'm not a negative person. I was thinking, 'You never know,' because they were a great troop and had a great team spirit about them. I'm not pretending it was the classiest City side ever, but we had a mixture of senior pros and younger players, and they were all together.

"I knew that togetherness would take us a long way. And then penalties... bloody penalties. I'd lost in the play-offs with Oldham so I didn't have particularly good memories of the play-offs. We'd lost on away goals then. So I started worrying slightly when it went to a penalty shoot-out.

"We'd been practising penalties and Nicky Weaver hadn't got near too many. He was going to be an England goalkeeper but for injuries and distractions. He wasn't great at penalties – but it's a different thing. A lot of good penalty stoppers haven't necessarily been great goalkeepers and vice versa. Peter Shilton – who was the best I ever played with – wasn't great at penalties.

"And then Nicky went on to stop two and they blazed a third over. His celebrations will long be remembered."

Royle also says he was surprised at the person who missed City's only unsuccessful kick: "In all the penalty practices we had, Dicky had been comfortably the best penalty taker. He's a great guy, totally committed and a completely different person on the pitch – when he's crossed the white line, he thinks he's six foot five! When I joined City, he wasn't a bad kicker of the ball, but he was an over-

"When Kevin [Horlock] scored, I can't say I felt like we'd do it, but I wasn't feeling negative because I'm not a negative person. I was thinking, 'You never know,' because they were a great troop and had a great team spirit about them."

excitable kicker of it. He used to get into great positions and then try and smash it into the back of the net.

"I said to him, 'Calm down and concentrate on hitting the target – you won't score unless you hit the target' and when his big chance came [in the Play-Off Final], he side-footed it," Royle says. "I'd like to think prior to my arrival he might have blasted it and possibly missed the target. He didn't, it was controlled and he got us there.

"So, when it came to penalties, I was very confident with Dicky," he says, "and then he went and hit both posts and it didn't go in. I've never seen that before.

"The coach home was quiet. One of the first things that happened was David Bernstein came up to me after the game and said, 'I've had contact from the town hall – they want to know if we'll do an open top bus tour next week.' I said no. Manchester City celebrating coming out of the third tier isn't right."

The day before the game saw one moment that illustrated the team spirit in the squad that season. Royle explains what happened: "We'd arrived at the hotel and there was the most torrential downpour you've ever seen. Kevin Horlock – who was, and still is, marvellously insane – was having a contest with Jeff Whitley to see who could stand outside the hotel the longest in this tropical rain. We're all just looking on from under the cover of the reception just wetting ourselves at these two idiots seeing who can stand out in the rain for long enough.

"It was daft stuff," he continues, "it was boy stuff. It was all part of the pressure relief. They had a great camaraderie."

When Royle joined City, in February 1998, the Blues were in a precarious position in Division One. The club had 14 games of the season remaining and were second bottom in the league, having won just seven matches all campaign. Succeeding Frank Clark, Royle explains what it was like when he first walked through the door.

"It was muddled," he says. "It was a club in turmoil. There were too many players that shouldn't have been there, really. They'd had a succession of managers who had all brought players in, but hadn't been able to get rid of players. We had over 50 pros when I got there – and the sorts of players that time had forgotten. The first deadline day was spent in the boardroom just letting players out on loan or on frees just to reduce the wage bill. It's no secret we were financially bereft.

"When I signed the contract there, the board didn't know who was going to be in charge come the new season," he continues, "they didn't even know if they would still be there or even if the club was going to go into liquidation. They offered me a contract that lasted until the end of the season.

"I said, 'Well, I've no problem with that personally, but I don't think it's what the fans want to hear. So I think the best thing would be to tell me that I've got a three year contract, but have a clause in it where either party can cancel it at the end of the season.' And that's what we did – by the end of the season, they were happy with what they'd seen and wanted me to stay on.

"It was a club in turmoil. There were too many players that shouldn't have been there, really. They'd had a succession of managers who had all brought players in, but hadn't been able to get rid of players. We had over 50 pros when I got there..."

"The first job was to avoid relegation," he continues, "which we narrowly missed. Again, in true City style, we had to win on the last game of the season – which we did – and one or two results had to go for us, but everything went against us. But, after that, there was a lot of sorting out to do. The position with Gio [Kinkladze] and other players who were under contract, but shouldn't have been there, the whole thing needed trimming, economising and starting again."

To give some idea of how bad things were at Manchester City when the former City striker took up the position in the Blues' dugout, the fans held up a banner before kick-off of his very first match. The supporters knew their side's future was in jeopardy and responded with the words, 'Mr Royle, please, please save our club'.

There can be little argument about the influence Royle had on the club. Working with chairman David Bernstein, he managed to reduce the wage bill to a manageable level, he reduced the size of the squad and created a team with harmony in the dressing room, and, on top of all of that, he dug the club out of the hole that it had fallen into. He got everybody pulling in the same direction and – albeit it with a couple of scares along the way – earned successive promotions, catapulting the Blues back into the Premier League earlier than most were expecting.

He tells me the fans' reactions to him even today are still humbling: "I'm always very conscious when I go to Manchester to speak to and meet fans, there's generally a great respect. It's a nice feeling that people think that, but I don't really think of it in that way personally – and I don't say that in false modesty!

"Somebody said to me after Gillingham, 'Did you ever think of the consequences had we lost that game?' The answer was no. The biggest thing was that the fans had stayed with us for that season – everywhere we went, we broke records with the away fans.

"I don't know that the fans would have stayed with us to that extent for another season," he continues, "I like to think they would. I always say the City fans are the best in the business because no other club of their size has had to endure the pain and the anguish that they have, and they've stood by it. Whether or not that would have gone on into a second season [in the third tier], I don't know."

Royle was under pressure from the fans from the start of his first full campaign in charge. Having been relegated, the Blues were favourites for the Division Two title, but the start to the season left that possibility well out of reach by the beginning of winter. Languishing in mid-table, some fans were beginning to question whether Royle was the right man for the job. Quickly, though, he proved that he was – and produced a second half of the season run of form that one would expect from title contenders (though, in this case, it was only enough to make a push for second place).

"We got to grips with the division," the ex-manager says, "we came to terms with every game at Maine Road being the biggest game of the season for the visiting side – more so than their home game because Maine Road was a stadium they might never play on again. It was a hard division, but we had goalscorers so I always felt that gave us a chance.

"I always say the City fans are the best in the business because no other club of their size has had to endure the pain and the anguish that they have, and they've stood by it."

"When Andy Morrison came, although there wasn't an immediate renaissance, his influence was still felt when he wasn't playing. In the nicest of terms and I don't mean this in any negative way, but Andy was a bit of a bully and that's what the club needed. We signed him for his personality and to be the captain, as much as we signed him for the player. And he was a better player than people realise, but he'd just – if you've read his book – had a chequered life and but for that he would have had many Scottish caps. There were centre halves playing for Scotland in his time that weren't as good as him."

After returning to Division One at the first attempt, Royle tells me that the club's aim was to hold their position and remain in the second tier. Having only just escaped Division Two, few were expecting what happened next – and Royle explains that the eventual outcome of winning automatic promotion exceeded even what he was anticipating.

"We had the preseason meeting with the board," he says, "first, we acknowledged what had just happened with a big smile and a big sigh, and then we talked about prospects for the future and what we needed to consolidate. One of the board asked me how I felt we could do and I said, 'Don't rule us out of the play-offs.' That certainly turned one or two heads – they didn't think that we were anywhere near that.

"I thought we were high on spirit and if we could get a little bit more width in to supply Goater – which came in the form of Mark Kennedy – then I thought we could have a go at it. And, whilst I'm sure they appreciated the bravado and the confidence, one or two certainly thought I was slightly puzzled."

Royle says that winning games became a habit: "There was a bounce effect," he explains, "you see clubs come up and initially do very well, so it was whether we could last it out. Through the season, we maintained a level of consistency that was pretty good. When it came to the run-in, I was confident – just a bit wary of Cityitis. But this time it came from the fans when they all ran on the pitch [after a home win against Birmingham], thinking it was done and it wasn't!"

Following the Blues' 1-0 win at home to Birmingham, the club was sitting in second place on 86 points with one fixture left to play. Ipswich were five points behind in third, but had a game in hand, meaning the Tractor Boys had to win both matches and hope City lost on the final day to stand any chance of the automatic promotion slot. The pitch invasion came because Ipswich's next game was an away tie with league champions Charlton – who had only lost four at home all season.

In typical City style, Ipswich won.

Worse, at half time on the final day of the season, they were beating Walsall at Portman Road, while City were losing at Blackburn – Rovers had hit the woodwork several times in the first half and had battered City into the ground, but had only found the net once. Had results stayed the way they were, it was the Suffolk team who would finish second and City would have had another year of play-offs.

"We sat down at half time," Royle says, "and I said to the players 'This isn't us. We're lucky we're still in this. But don't forget something that we have behind us is that we always score. We're only 1-0 down and we always score.'

"And then soon after half time, they hit the post again and it came back and dropped into Nicky Weaver's arms and I turned to Asa [Hartford] and said, 'There's something going on here, this could be our day!' I honestly felt that, but I didn't expect us to run out 4-1 winners."

Royle then explains to me how that game almost saw Maine Road kitted out with some new equipment: "One of my greatest friends in football had been a young secretary at Oldham when I started there," he says. "Tom Finn was then on the board at Blackburn and I met him in the close season and he was genuinely pleased for us that we'd gone up – though I don't think he could tell Graeme Souness [Blackburn's manager at the time] that.

"And after a few drinks, I tried to buy the posts and crossbars at Ewood Park off him," he says, laughing, "I won't say he got irate, but he told me where to go!"

That victory sent the club back to the top flight – where, despite a spirited start to the season, the Blues ultimately fell short of what was required to stay in the league.

"Tom Finn [a friend of Royle's from Oldham] was then on the board at Blackburn... And after a few drinks, I tried to buy the posts and crossbars at Ewood Park off him."

Over the course of the season, wins were hard to come by – with City earning just eight in the 38 matches of the campaign.

"You can never say a promotion was too early," Royle tells me when I ask if he thinks the club wasn't ready for the Premier League, "it comes when it comes and the sooner the better. It was possibly too early for us financially – when you look and see the spending after me, under Keegan, or with Hughes, Mancini or Pellegrini, you'd have to say the club was probably under-funded then. But we did bring players in.

"It's a hard one when you're promoted," he continues, "because you've got a group of players, particularly after two promotions, who have got you there. They were high on spirit, not short on ability, but some of them were kids who were unproven at that level. We had a group of players who loved the club, but we needed players of proven ability in the Premier League. I brought in George Weah, Paulo Wanchope, Steve Howey – none of who were particularly expensive buys, but were all experienced.

"We started off ok," he continues. "I don't know how or why the George Weah thing [his sudden departure from Maine Road] affected us, but it did. It caught us out and it certainly affected Paulo Wanchope, who was in awe of him. I don't know how much influence he had over him, but it was never quite the same with Paulo after George had gone.

"We had a game that I didn't particularly want George to play in," Royle explains, "I didn't want to upset him and I tried to explain that I thought it was a game too far for him. He looked tired and he was tired, so he shouldn't have started. Equally, though, I didn't want to take away his belief. He was getting on; he was 33 or 34 and an ex-Footballer of the Year, so you have to give him that respect.

> "There was a month where everything that could have gone wrong went wrong for us. Danny Tiatto scored a goal at Middlesbrough when he ran past player after player from the halfway line and it was disallowed for Darren Huckerby standing offside..."

"We came in at half time and there was shouting," he says, "he later said I swore at him, but it was another member of staff who did that. We were all getting very angry and frustrated at the time.

"Then, all of a sudden, we got the news from his agent that he wanted to go and that he had a move fixed up in France," the ex-manager explains, "and this was in two days. So whether or not he'd seen this coming and had arranged a move to France, I don't know. I don't know whether he became disillusioned and somebody cottoned on to it and asked him to go to France. I respected his talent so much, but it was his fitness levels that were down and were never going to be the same because of his age.

"Andy Morrison had his continuing knee problems, Richard Jobson was still playing when he had no right to be – his ankle was that bad that he was a hero every time he put his boots on for us – and the Goat scored goals. But all round, we didn't quite hack it. Whether we should have spent more or spent differently, it doesn't really matter. The bottom line was that we didn't do it.

"There was a month where everything that could have gone wrong went wrong for us," he says, "Danny Tiatto scored a goal at Middlesbrough when he ran past player after player from the halfway line and it was disallowed for Darren Huckerby standing offside on the other side of the pitch. Then we had a goal disallowed against Tottenham for no reason at all and they went to the other end and scored in the last minute. And that's when you start thinking that maybe Lady Luck's decided that this isn't going to be for us, this year."

The former manager also explains that it was a difficult time for him off the pitch as well as for the team on it: "Personally, my wife was ill," he says, "she had cancer. My father also had emphysema and cancer and it was a hard time, there's no doubt about that."

At the end of the season, the Blues were relegated a year to the day after winning promotion at Ewood Park. In another City-only coincidence, it was Ipswich who put the final nail in the club's Premier League coffin, having been promoted themselves through the play-offs and doing better than anyone expected they would. They earned a UEFA Cup spot with a fifth place finish.

The result meant that, whatever City did against Chelsea on the final day, they couldn't escape the bottom three. With the pressure off, the Blues played well, but, as was the story of their season, didn't take their chances and succumbed to a 2-1 defeat.

Royle was sacked in the summer.

I ask him if the decision to relieve him of his duties came as a shock: "It did only because I'd met with Bernstein the previous week," he says, "I'd always got on very well with him and did until the day I left. I think he was a terrific chairman and I think being without Bernstein was a mistake by City [when the chairman later resigned over the signing of Robbie Fowler].

"But I'd met him the previous week in a restaurant in the Curry Mile [Manchester's strip of Indian restaurants]," he continues, "and we had a good chat about things and about why we'd gone down. And he challenged my staff – he said he had great confidence and belief in me, but not in my staff and he intimated that he wanted me to sack Alex Stepney, John Hurst, Roy Bailey and even Asa Hartford maybe.

"And I said I disagreed because they were the same staff that had seen us go up two divisions. I said I thought we'd been caught out and that we'd not had the best of fortune – although every relegated manager says that – but I thought that if we'd had more money available to compete for the better players to make that quantum leap, we might just have done it.

"But I did say that I knew the team that was going down was a better one than the team that went up.

"We left that meeting to meet again on the Monday morning to discuss plans for the new season with, as I believed, John Wardle and David Makin," he continues, "but when I arrived, I found it was a full board meeting and when I went in I was told I was to be sacked. And that was that.

"As a relegated manager, you know that whatever you say there's no mitigation in relegation. You're down. If they wanted to sack me as the manager of a relegated side, I would have no objections. I wouldn't be happy with it, but I can see the point – the club wanting change. So when I started reading that we were a pub team and that sort of nonsense, it wasn't nice.

"There were some rather bad insinuations coming out from behind the scenes and I know where it was coming from. Quite honestly, it wasn't nice because the pub team had been promoted twice in three years as well. There's another side to City – there's the Cityitis, which is true. But equally true is that they don't always do things nicely or properly and I felt they hadn't done this right.

"The galling part really was that, as soon as Keegan took over, they started spending money on the grounds that they wouldn't spend when I was there. They started spending money on players – they were looking at a different kind of player than we'd been able to afford. So that was a little bit galling, I have to say.

> **"If they wanted to sack me as the manager of a relegated side, I would have no objections. I wouldn't be happy with it, but I can see the point – the club wanting change. So when I started reading that we were a pub team and that sort of nonsense, it wasn't nice."**

"But I've got nothing but affection for Manchester City as both a player and a manager. I've got great friends there and it's a wonderful club that has a great feel behind it and a great tradition. And I'm delighted for what's happening there now."

On that point, I suggest to Royle that it was his groundwork that laid the foundations for the club to be seen as investable by the likes of the Abu Dhabi United Group, but he dismisses the suggestion completely. "I will accept," he says, "that the Gillingham game was very, very important in City's history – probably the most important because you just don't know where it would have gone had they had to spend another season in that division.

"The platform for the modern success came with money – as it did with all clubs. In 1963, Everton were the Merseyside Millionaires. Then

Arsenal, Manchester United, Liverpool... they've all had their spell of being big spenders and being successful. And not to forget Blackburn Rovers, who were big spenders for three years and won the Premier League as a result.

"Let's just say we put a support under the club when it was badly needed," he concludes, "and I'm proud of that. It was a lovely time in my life, with great memories.

"Sad memories, too, but overall it was a great time."